CORRIS RAILWAY

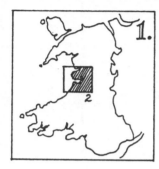

1.

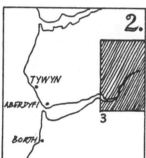

2.

TYWYN

ABERDYFI

BORTH

3.

CYMERAU

HENGAE

ABERLLEFENNI

ABERCORRIS — MATTHEW'S MILL

ABERCWMEIDDEW — GARNEDDWEN

GAEWERN — CORRIS
BRAICHGOCH

ERA

MAESPOETH Jⁿ — CAMBRIA WYNNE
PONT IFANS
ESGAIRGEILIOG — RHIWGWREIDDYN

LLWYNGWERN

LLWYNGWERN
LLIWDY
ABERGARFAN — DOLDDERWEN

FFRIDD GATE

MACHYNLLETH

DERWENLAS

CEI WARD

MORBEN

GLANDOVEY
Later Dyfi Junction

CEI COCH
(GARREG)

N

LEGEND

~·~·~	QUARRY
▬▬▬	LOCOMOTIVE OPERATED LINE
●—●	STATIONS
—+—	HALTS
▬ ▬ ▬	TRAMWAYS
▭ ▭ ▭	PROPOSED TRAMWAY
———	STANDARD-GAUGE
✕	LEVEL CROSSING

GREAT WESTERN CORRIS

Great Western CORRIS

Gwyn Briwnant-Jones

GOMER

First impression—July 1994

© Gwyn Briwnant-Jones

ISBN 1 85902 079 8

Printed by J. D. Lewis and Sons Ltd., Gomer Press, Llandysul, Dyfed

Acknowledgements

Few books of railway history are the result of individual effort; *Great Western Corris* is no exception. I am pleased, therefore, to record my appreciation of assistance readily and freely given by the following friends:

Dr Stuart Owen-Jones, Keeper of the Welsh Industrial & Maritime Museum, Cardiff, in addition to preparing a Foreword, has allowed me to draw upon the excellent and ever-increasing collection of material now in the museum's care; Michael Scott Archer generously loaned original copies of Parliamentary Plans & Sections for the Shrewsbury & Aberystwyth Railway (1852) and the Corris, Machynlleth & River Dovey Railway (1857)—details of gradients and distances quoted in the text, together with much other information, are from these sources. The onerous task of reading the manuscript was undertaken by Mr W. B. Jones, and I am indebted to him for his interest, encouragement and valued suggestions.

C. C. Green MBE; R. S. Greenhough; Ifor A. Higgon; T. Alfred Hughes; Islwyn M. Jones; Roger W. Kidner; Luther Morgans; R. C. Riley; R. and J. Swetman; and Dr Ralph Tutton all helped in various ways, either filling some of the gaps in my knowledge or kindly lending photographs from their collections. Individual photographers, where they are known, are usually credited beneath each image.

Final thanks go to members of my family for constant encouragement over many years. On this occasion my mother, particularly, has dealt with a great number of queries regarding her recollections of the Corris Railway and some of the personalities who worked the line.

Any errors which may have crept inadvertently into the text, however, are entirely my own responsibility.

Gwyn Briwnant-Jones   *Llangollen 1993*

Abbreviations used in the text.

BR	— British Railways
CRS	— Corris Railway Society
GWR	— Great Western Railway
N & M	— Newtown & Machynlleth Railway
NLW	— National Library of Wales, Aberystwyth
MPD	— Motive Power Depot
PRO	— Public Record Office, Kew
TR	— Tal-y-llyn Railway
TRPS	— Tal-y-llyn Railway Preservation Society
WIMM	— Welsh Industrial & Maritime Museum, Cardiff

Contents

Foreword

While a large number of railway histories now exist, relatively few historians have been able to base their accounts on extensive first-hand experience. This applies particularly to the narrow-gauge railways and to the rural branch lines which performed their daily routines largely unnoticed until they quietly faded away. The account given here by Gwyn Briwnant-Jones of the Corris Railway's Great Western phase is distinguished by the author's first-hand acquaintance with the railway. While not explicitly stated, the descriptions, nevertheless, have that underlying resonance of authenticity which characterises an author who totally understands and is in harmony with his subject. At the same time, this feeling of empathy is reinforced by the personal knowledge which allows the author to make the characters of those who worked on the railway in its latter days come alive in a most expressive manner.

This personal touch contributes greatly to the appeal of the book but it also has a wider significance. It is important for the sake of posterity that such memories are recorded, for, whether expressed in the first or the third person, the way of life and the method of operating are from a bygone era and the railway of the present day, let alone that of the future, has no place for events such as those described herein.

Stuart Owen-Jones
September 1993

CORRIS RAILWAY.

Time Table

FOR AUGUST, 1883,

AND UNTIL FURTHER NOTICE

The Times shown on this Bill are the Times at which the Trains are intended to arrive at and depart from the several Stations, but the Company cannot guarantee these times being kept, under all circumstances, nor will they be accountable for any loss, inconvenience, or injury, that may arise from delay or detention.

TICKETS must be shewn to the Company's Servants. or delivered up to them when demanded. They are only available on the day of issue.

CHILDREN'S TICKETS.—Children under Three years of age are conveyed Free, and those above three and under Twelve, Half-Price.

PASSENGERS' LUGGAGE.—The Company are not responsible for Luggage, unless it is Booked and Paid for according to its value. Each First Class Passenger is allowed 120 lbs. and each Third Class Passenger 60 lbs. weight of Luggage free of charge, the same not being Merchandise, or other articles for hire or profit. An excess above those weights will be charged.

RETURN TICKETS are only available on the day of issue.

NO SUNDAY TRAINS.

ALL TRAINS ARE FIRST CLASS AND PARLIAMENTARY.

			A a.m.	a.m.	p.m.	B p.m.	p.m.
Corris Railway.	Corris .... dep.		5 55	7 25	12 40	4 0	5 50
	Machynlleth ..... arr.		6 25	7 50	1 5	4 30	6 15
	FARES— CORRIS TO MACHYNLLETH. First Class ... Single, -/10 " ... Return, 1/6 Parliamentary ... Single, -/5 " ... Return, -/9						

			A a.m.	a.m.	p.m.	B p.m.	p.m.
CAMBRIAN RAILWAYS.	Machynlleth ..... dep.		....	8 0	1 16	5 25	6 25
	Aberdovey .... arr.		....	8 30	1 53	....	7 8
	Towyn ..... ,,		....	8 38	2 1	6 0	7 16
	Dolgelley ..... ,,		....	10 15	3 30	7 25	8 40
	Barmouth ..... ,,		....	9 20	2 40	6 35	7 55
	Machynlleth ..... dep.		6 33	9 20	1 16	5 20	6 25
	Borth .... arr.		7 4	9 59	1 59	5 45	7 8
	Aberystwith ..... ,,		7 25	10 20	2 27	6 0	7 30
	Machynlleth ..... dep.		8 35	9 50	1 40	...	7 0
	Newtown ..... arr.		10 7	10 56	2 57	...	8 15
	Welshpool .... ,,		10 50	11 23	3 28	...	8 50
	Whitchurch ..... ,,		....	12 30	5 10	...	10 15
L. & N. W. Rly.	Crewe .... arr.		....	1 5	6 5	...	11 0
	Birkenhead.... ..... ,,		....	2 45	7 46	...	3 5
	Liverpool (Lime Street) ,,		....	2 15	7 15	...	12 0
	Manchester (London Rd),,		....	2 25	7 25	...	12 50
	Shrewsbury ... arr.		....	12 30	4 51	...	9 50
	Stafford ..... ,,		....	1 30	6 35	...	11 4
	Birmingham (New St.) ,,		....	2 30	8 0	...	2 10
	London (Euston) ..... ,,		....	4 55	10 5	...	4 35

			p.m.		a.m.		a.m.
L. & N. W. Ry.	London (Euston) ..... dep.		9 15	....	5 15	....	10 30
	Birmingham (New Street) ,,		10 30	....	7 25	....	12 40
	Stafford ,,		2 13	....	8 55	....	1 55
	Shrewsbury ,,		3 20	....	10 30	....	2 55
	Manchester (London Rd)dep.		11 20	....	7 15	10 0	11 45
	Liverpool (Lime Street) ,,		11 10	....	7 20	9 45	11 45
	Birkenhead ,,		....	....	8 20	10 10	11 40
	Crewe.... ,,		....	....	8 40	11 5	1 5

			a.m.	a.m.			
CAMBRIAN RAILWAYS.	Whitchurch ..... dep.		....	....	9 50	12 0	1 50
	Welshpool ,,		4 40	....	11 28	1 20	3 45
	Newtown ,,		5 16	....	12 4	1 49	4 12
	Machynlleth ..... arr.		6 30	....	1 14	3 12	5 17
	Aberystwith ..... dep.		....	8 45	12 40	....	6 0
	Borth ..... ,,		....	9 1	1 1	....	6 22
	Machynlleth ..... arr.		....	9 40	1 38	....	6 56
	Barmouth ..... dep.		....	8 35	12 10	....	5 28
	Dolgelley ..... ,,		....	7 55	12 0	....	5 9
	Towyn ..... ,,		....	9 12	12 54	....	6 4
	Aberdovey ..... ,,		....	7 55	1 3	....	6 14
	Machynlleth ..... arr.		....	9 45	1 38	....	6 46

			A a.m.	a.m.	p.m.	C p.m.	p.m.
Corris Railway.	Machynlleth ..... dep.		6 35	9 50	1 50	5 0	7 5
	Corris ..... arr.		7 0	10 15	2 20	5 30	7 30
	FARES MACHYNLLETH TO CORRIS. First Class ... Single, -/10 " ... Return, 1/6 Parliamentary ... Single, -/5 " ... Return, -/9						

A—On Mondays only. B—Saturdays only. C—Wednesdays and Saturdays only.

Tourists and others will find this the best and easiest way of reaching CADER IDRIS, and the famous TALYLLYN LAKE

MANAGER'S OFFICE,
Corris, July 24th, 1883.

J. R. DIX, Manager.

WOODALL & CO., Steam-Printers and Lithographer, Oswestry.

Introduction

The first rails to reach Machynlleth, situated just above the highest navigable point on the river Dyfi in mid Wales, were laid to a narrow gauge of 2ft 3ins for the purpose of transporting high-quality slates and slabs from the south Merionethshire quarries of the Corris district to the Dyfi river boats.

Constructed in 1858/9 as the Corris, Machynlleth & River Dovey Railway or Tramroad (*sic*), the tramway soon abbreviated its title to the more manageable 'Corris Railway', and improved its services and facilities in a similar, businesslike manner. It was always a most attractive line; indeed, many would claim that amongst the Welsh narrow gauge, it was second only to the mighty and much more famous Ffestiniog.

Its success was such that the Cambrian Railways contemplated taking over the line in 1894 but the Corris remained independent, even avoiding the Grouping of 1922/3, until it was acquired by the Great Western in 1930. It then formed part of a package deal wherein the most attractive components, undoubtedly, were tram and bus interests established principally in and around the City of Bristol, although the fact that the progressive little Corris had a thriving bus service of its own did not pass unnoticed at Paddington.

The Corris, however, was more than a railway which happened to be located in Wales; it was a thoroughly Welsh concern. With one or two exceptions, its employees were virtually all local people, unlike the neighbouring Cambrian Company which employed few Welshmen during the early years. The administration of the line, it is true, was conducted in English and for many years the headquarters were at Bristol or Paddington /Oswestry, but the language of the operators was Welsh, certainly during the present century. Undoubtedly, a considerable portion of the ebullient Mr Dix's success may be attributed to his capacity for getting things done at a local level and, in this respect, his ability to converse with the men in their own language proved a major factor.

When railways were introduced to Wales during the last century, the Welsh language was suppressed in educational spheres and saw little commercial use. Rule books and instructions were written in English and although Welsh was used orally by many of the staff, English technical terms were freely adopted or adapted. Over a century later, Welsh people are somewhat more reluctant to borrow terms so readily and there seems little doubt that if railways were being introduced to Wales today, a new colloquial vocabulary would evolve around them, as has happened to a degree with other technical developments, such as computers and television.

In the nineteenth century, however, the vocabulary of the day-to-day Welsh speaker incorporated many corruptions of English terms. Verbs were lazily adapted by adding '-io' to the English version, e.g., *shyntio, bwcio, stampio*, whilst railway nouns like signals, points or carriage were adopted *en bloc*, although it must be stated that English terms were used almost universally during the development of railways. [1]

It may be appropriate, therefore, to highlight a few English words found within the text which were rarely used colloquially by the people of the district. The most obvious example, perhaps, will be driver Humphreys's name. The formal and correct Humphrey Humphreys is used herein—it more befits the printed format—but the driver was always known as *Wmffre*, and the use of Humphrey will appear alien to many Welsh-speaking persons.

The word 'wagon' appeared in official documents (usually spelt with two g's) but was rarely used orally. The normal Corris term was 'dram' which may merely have been the Welsh version of 'tram', although 'dram' featured in the first Standing Order related to railways passed by the House of Commons in 1799, when it appeared as a proper English word in relation to Dram Roads. [2] If, perchance, the term 'wagon' was used orally on the Corris, it was always pronounced 'wagen'.

'*Yr injan*'—the engine—is obviously a borrowed term perpetuated to this day in railway circles where Welsh is spoken, whilst on the Corris, reference was always to '*yr injan fêch*'—the little engine—pronounced with the flat 'e' so characteristic of the Montgomeryshire/south Merionethshire Welsh dialect.

The terms 'up' and 'down', in a railway context, usually indicate the direction of travel up to or down from London. Welsh valley lines, however, generally disregard the practice and consider 'up' to refer to travel up a valley to its source, thus the terms are frequently used within the text as a concise indication of the direction of travel.

Great Western Corris does not purport to be a complete account of the railway's history, but seeks to portray the post-1930 period and is based largely upon personal observation and photographs. A few of the latter are of such indifferent quality that they would not normally be considered,

but they are included here because of their content. The initial chapter serves mainly to set the scene for those who may be unfamiliar with the line's topography and early development, but the opportunity is also taken to present relevant 'new' information originally gleaned during research for *Railway Through Talerddig*. By its very nature much of this is incomplete but such material, together with appropriate references, will hopefully serve to guide others toward a definitive account. No attempt is made to repeat information which has already been presented in previous publications: readers who require such detail are referred to the Bibliography.

Introduction: Notes & References

[1] Professor Jack Simmons (1991) *The Victorian Railway*, Thames & Hudson, pp. 174-194.
[2] *Railway Magazine*, March/April 1944, p. 81. 'Dram Roads' by Kenneth Brown.

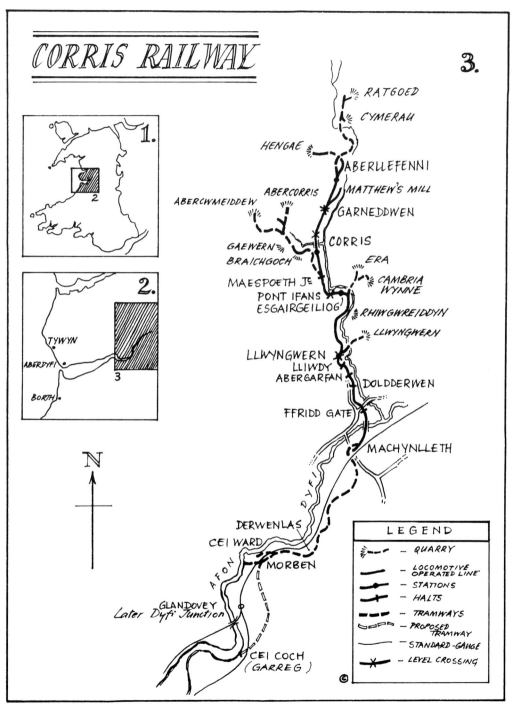

CORRIS RAILWAY

3.

1.

2

2.

TYWYN

ABERDYFI

BORTH

3

RATGOED

CYMERAU

HENGAE

ABERLLEFENNI

ABERCWMEIDDEW

ABERCORRIS

MATTHEW'S MILL

GARNEDDWEN

CORRIS

GAEWERN

BRAICHGOCH

ERA

CAMBRIA
WYNNE

MAESPOETH Jᵉ

PONT IFANS

ESGAIRGEILIOG

RHIWGWREIDDYN

LLWYNGWERN

LLWYNGWERN

LLIWDY

ABERGARFAN

DOLDDERWEN

FFRIDD GATE

MACHYNLLETH

DYFI

N

DERWENLAS

CEI WARD

MORBEN

AFON

GLANDOVEY
Later Dyfi Junction

CEI COCH
(GARREG)

LEGEND

	QUARRY
	LOCOMOTIVE OPERATED LINE
	STATIONS
	HALTS
	TRAMWAYS
	PROPOSED TRAMWAY
	STANDARD-GAUGE
	LEVEL CROSSING

Chapter 1

The Days of Prosperity

General topography, and its influence on early working practices.

There is evidence that sporadic quarrying of slate has taken place in the Aberllefenni district of south Merionethshire since 1500, although the industry was not really established in the area until the nineteenth century with the re-opening of the Aberllefenni quarry in 1810, the Gaewern quarry in 1820 and the Braich-goch quarry in 1835: the latter two eventually combined to form one of the largest quarries in the district. The 'Braich' or 'Tynno', as it was often referred to locally, survived until 1971; the Aberllefenni quarry, the sole survivor, still produces high quality slabs at the time of writing (summer 1993).

The quarries located near the southern boundary of the old county of Merioneth owed their existence to rich veins of slate which run almost directly on a true north-east/south-west axis from near Dinas Mawddwy, inland, to the coast near Tywyn. It is no accident that a ruler placed on a map of the region reveals that the quarries at Minllyn, near Dinas Mawddwy, Maesygamfa and Hendre Ddu above Aberangell; those at Aberllefenni, Cymerau and Ratgoed; the Upper Corris complex of Ty'n-y-ceunant, Gaewern, Abercwmeiddew and Abercorris; and finally Bryneglwys (above Abergynolwyn), are almost in line with one another.

The quality of the slate varies from indifferent to excellent, borne out on the one hand by the numerous trial pits sunk and abandoned during the last century, and by the fact that there remains, still, a demand for the very best quality, exemplified by the Aberllefenni slabs.

During the early period, the output of the Aberllefenni and Corris quarries was transported in panniers or horse-drawn carts to the nearest navigable water, at Derwen-las on the river Dyfi, some 8-9 miles away. Here, the slates were loaded into river boats for local distribution, or tran-

During a visit to the Upper Corris area in 1957, the Kidner family discovered an interesting piece of fish-belly rail. This is much rarer in the Corris area than bridge rail, and probably pre-dates the CM&RDT. After consulting David Bick and Dr. Lewis of Hull University, Roger Kidner is of the opinion that this rail came from the Gaewern quarry incline and, according to a reference in the *Caernarvon & Denbigh Herald* of 15 August 1836, railways had existed at Gaewern before that date!

Roger W. Kidner, 1957

shipped again at nearby Aberdyfi into sturdier, sea-going vessels for export further afield.

The system worked fairly well until escalating demand accentuated the inadequate transport link between quarries and river. Initial efforts to construct a tramway to the water's edge—the first dating from 1850—proved unsuccessful but the quarry owners, led by Earl Vane, of Plas Machynlleth (Braich-goch quarry) and R. D. Pryce, of Cyfronydd (Aberllefenni quarry), eventually succeeded in obtaining Parliamentary approval for the construction of a horse-drawn tramway. This 1858 scheme, for a narrow-gauge line via Machynlleth to Cei Coch, near Glandyfi, was later amended and the tramway may not, in fact,

The village of Corris in a D & S George Real Photograph. The card was used postally from Machynlleth in 1938, but obviously predates that time.

Braichgoch Inn is visible alongside the main road (lower L/H corner) and the sprawling waste tips of the Braichgoch and Gaewern quarries dominate the area above, whilst those of the Abercwmeiddew quarry are prominent in the centre background. The village of Corris occupies the lower R/H foreground and an original card, viewed carefully, reveals the station area to be in good order. All glass roofs are intact and a row of wagons stands in the loop; an open-topped charabanc is parked hard against the rear of the station.

Few figures are evident in the whole panorama; gardens and allotments, for example, are trim but unattended, giving the impression of a tranquil, even hot, summer's afternoon: it all possesses something of the air of the Sabbath, were it not for some washing drying at Pentre Farm and at Frongaled.

The majestic Cader Idris is visible in the hazy distance. c. 1925.

George & Son 'Real Photograph Series'

have extended much further downstream than Cei Ward, at Morben.[1]

The downward gradient between Ratgoed, the most northerly quarry in the region, and Machynlleth was continuous, although variable, leading naturally to the supposition that loaded trains were always worked down by gravity, with horses used to return the empty wagons to the quarries. As there is no evidence, to date, to suggest that 'dandy cars', used for transporting horses on the downward 'gravity' runs on the Ffestiniog, for example, were ever operated on the Corris, it

would seem that the horses returned to Machynlleth on the adjacent road whilst the slates and slabs went ahead, by gravity.

It is equally possible, however, that horses may have worked loaded trains in the 'down' direction also, particularly during the earliest period. This supposition is supported by what is regarded as the earliest known image of a Corris train, featured in *A Return to Corris*[2] in which two horses are depicted working in the 'down' direction near Braich-goch.

2

The original intention may well have been to operate 'down' trains only by gravity, but experience at the outset could have brought some unexpected problems, for certain sections of the run, particularly that from Pantperthog (near Llwyn-gwern) to Abergarfan, called for considerable skill on the part of the travelling brakesmen to judge the speed correctly and avoid the extremes of stalling or derailment. The gradient on this section was comparatively gentle—at 1 in 550, the nearest to level track between Aberllefenni and the Dyfi river bridge, but the main problem was created by the sharp curve at Pantperthog, at the entry to this section for south-bound runs. This effectively restricted brakesmen from fully using any momentum gained from the preceding 1 in 53. There was no problem when the run was in experienced hands and under normal weather conditions, but an overcautious approach to the Pantperthog curve or the effect of a strong head wind on the ensuing run to Abergarfan could reduce momentum and bring the run to a halt. In later years, when the Mail wagon was prone to stall in this sector, it was usually possible to push the wagon to Doldderwen and gain a better gradient, but such a remedy was obviously not feasible with a heavy run of slabs. The introduction of gravity power may, therefore, have been a more gradual process, born of a combination of experiment and experience, than is sometimes assumed.

However, the final gradient of any note, from Ffridd Gate to Machynlleth, was ideal for gravity working, as the combination of inclined plane and a straight run ensured that any loads released at Ffridd Gate could be allowed to coast freely, with minimum attention, virtually to Machynlleth, where the convenient provision of stables suggests that fresh horses would have been available to move the train promptly on to Derwen-las. In this instance, operation by gravity would clearly have been far easier than horse-haulage.

Very few details are known of the operations of the horse tramway era and it must be emphasised that some of the foregoing, although not entirely without credence, is partly supposition; hopefully, more positive information may emerge one day.

The village of Pantperthog has changed little over the years. This postcard, from the Park Series of Newtown, was used postally in 1924 but its origins could easily pre-date that time by a decade or more. The 1 in 53 gradient on the railway at this point is apparent by comparing the inclination of the track in front of the cottages and a datum level represented by the roof line of the village school, in the centre of the composition. There is little wonder that the station was located at nearby Llwyngwern. c. 1900.

Park Series, Newtown

Llwyngwern station, looking south towards Pantperthog (around the curve). The minor road led to Plas Llwyngwern and to Llwyngwern quarry, now the Centre for Alternative Technology. The tramway from the quarry trailed into the picture from the left, passing behind the station building before joining the main line. Note the absence of cats' eyes and road markings on the narrow carriage-way at this date. 5.7.1936.

S. W. Baker

One of the small steel-sided wagons was designated for mail traffic. It would frequently be attached behind the last carriage on 'up' journeys and for this reason, had a special bracket on the Machynlleth end for attaching a lamp. Although it was not used for this purpose after the late '20s, the bracket remained in place until 1948. The other end of the wagon, clearly visible in the photograph, could be dropped down for easier loading of heavy objects.

'Down' journeys were usually successfully undertaken by gravity although there were occasions when high winds, snow or obstructions on the line caused the mail wagon to be 'marooned' and rescued by the engine. The words 'Corris Railway' appear to have been stencilled fairly liberally, considering the small area involved. They surmounted the main lettering and are also just discernable on the right-hand, sunlit panel, applied diagonally.

G. H. W. Clifford, courtesy C. C. Green

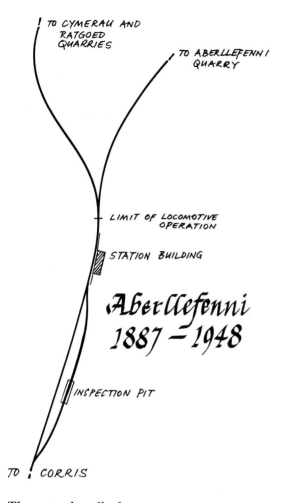

TO CYMERAU AND
RATGOED
QUARRIES

TO ABERLLEFENNI
QUARRY

LIMIT OF LOCOMOTIVE
OPERATION

STATION BUILDING

*Aberllefenni
1887 – 1948*

INSPECTION PIT

TO CORRIS

roughly hewn stone would be sawn or split according to its nature and the demand, and the finished products loaded onto the narrow-gauge wagons for transportation to the coast. The tramway for this purpose was single throughout and of necessity followed a tortuous course to ensure a gradual declination towards sea level.

Commencing at Ratgoed, the route to Aberllefenni passed the site of Cymerau quarry on the left side as it traversed the remote and rather wild terrain near the head of the valley. This section of the tramway, which was always horse/gravity worked, incorporated some severe curves which would not have tolerated a steam engine without

Aberllefenni quarry was noted for some remarkable inclines.

Above, a good though rather distant view is obtained of the trestle carriage which carried a narrow-gauge wagon at right-angles to the main incline. This ran on a wider gauge than the tramway's 2 ft 3 ins. This latter gauge was utilised alongside, however, for the balancing ballast wagon which ran directly down the incline. The condition of both sets of track would appear to give rise for considerable concern as, indeed, might the rails emanating from the lower adit! 1970.

R. W. Kidner

The route described

As the line's purpose was the carriage of slate and slabs from the quarries to the sea, the route is described in that direction, using the quarries at Ratgoed/Aberllefenni as a starting point, although all mileage quoted is from Machynlleth.

Some slate in the area was mined underground, but most was quarried on exposed mountainsides which were frequently windswept and rainlashed. The journey usually commenced when a small loaded wagon was lowered dramatically down an incline, or series of inclines, to the machine sheds, called Tŷ'r Injan (Engine House), perhaps many hundreds of feet lower down the hillside. Here the

This view shows a shorter incline of wide gauge track in which the empty wagon on the trestle is almost hidden from view at the foot of the left hand incline, whilst the balancing vehicle at the top of the opposite incline carries a water tank which was filled at the summit from the feed-pipe, just discernible, and emptied after it had travelled to the lower lever. 8.8.1960.

WIMM

obvious re-laying and considerable, and expensive, easement.

Some two miles south of Ratgoed, the tramway crossed over another branch coming in from the Aberllefenni quarry in the Hengae valley. After serving the nearby machine sheds, this line effected a trailing junction with the Ratgoed branch, just before the iron rails of the combined tramways gave way to the steel rails of the locomotive-worked section to Machynlleth, at the commencement of the Corris Railway proper. This end-on junction was marked by a white gate across the rails.

Just beyond, a small, narrow station building was located on a low slate-edged platform, on the left-hand side. At 6½ m. from Machynlleth, this was the northern terminus of passenger operations at Aberllefenni. Immediately to the south of the narrow platform lay a loop line and inspection pit.

As the line meandered gently south past the village hall and Tan-y-coed, another trailing junction on the left marked the ingress of the long siding which sloped across the meadow and main road from Matthew's Mill, an enamelling factory which regularly sent its products by rail. Slabs suitable for mantelpieces, for example, were decorated and heated here at high temperatures and the simulated marble effects revealed workmanship of a high order. This locomotive-worked private siding was not lifted with the remainder of the Corris line in 1948/9 but survived a few further years before finding its way, like almost everything else of use at that time, to the Tal-y-llyn Railway.

A row of quarrymen's houses on the right and a gated level crossing were the most prominent features of Garnedd-wen (5¾ m.). The crossing was controlled by signals and there was at one time a small wooden waiting shed. Onwards to Corris, the train enjoyed some straight stretches of track, as it passed between examples of the slate fences for which the area was noted. The track was usually set into the slope of the terrain, on the right side of the valley. Moreover, as the clearance on this side was extremely tight for most of the journey, it made sense to have doors only on the opposite side of the train, thus all stations conformed to the practice and were all on the same (easterly) side of the track.

Corris, the next stop after Garnedd-wen, was the line's principal intermediate station. At the outskirts, a minor road was negotiated on the level before some backyard views of adjacent houses emphasised progress through the heart of the village. After crossing Afon Deri by means of a tall bridge built of slate waste, southbound travellers were brought directly into Corris station (5m.) with its low platform and over-all roof, the latter unique on the Welsh narrow gauge.

The exterior of the cutting and trimming sheds at Aberllefenni quarry in 1925. The quarry now produces slabs only and this building is still in use today, although the machinery has been considerably modernised and the external layout has been adapted to present-day methods of handling, storage and transport. The crude but effective single-blade point and wagon turntables, in the centre foreground, are noteworthy features, as are the flat cars loaded with newly won rock. 1925.

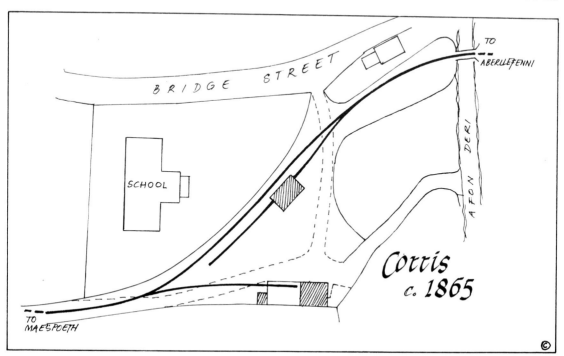

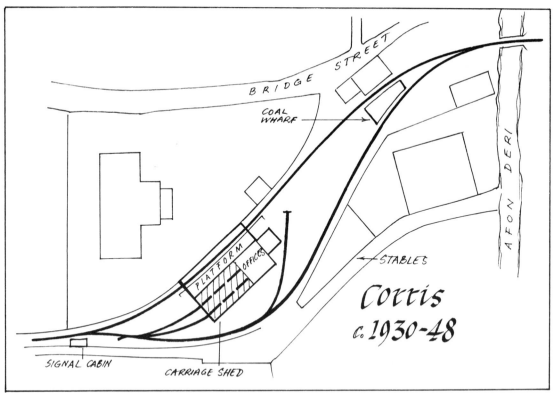

Corris station, showing clearly the low platform and overall roof on the left, with the adjacent two-road carriage shed and run-round loop. Part of the stable complex, (with the steeply pitched roof; background, extreme right) currently houses the Corris Railway Society's Museum.

This familiar view epitomises the period before the Great War when dividends were paid and rolling stock, track and infrastructure were in good order. 29.6.1909.

Ken Nunn Coll.

8

The approach to Corris, showing the Aberllefenni line curving to the left, the two-road carriage shed—already minus some of its roof glazing, and the goods loop with wagons on the right. The signal and cabin were reasonably intact considering they had been little used during the previous four years. 12.8.1935.

H. F. Wheeler, courtesy R. S. Carpenter

A run-round loop, end-loading siding, a two-road carriage shed, plus ground frame and signals were located here, as also were extensive stables for the many horses which either worked the line in the early days or later hauled the tourist coaches and wagonettes to Tal-y-llyn Lake. Indeed, a horse was stabled here by the GWR up to the closure of the line in 1948, for shunting at Aberllefenni or collection and delivery by cart in the Corris area.

Some of the stables are now refurbished and serve as the Corris Railway Society's Museum. The fact that 2ft 3ins track continues to wend its way between Corris and Maes-poeth is also attributable to the society, and it is hoped that trains may once again traverse this section, 'ere long', to use an optimistic phrase favoured by Victorian newspaper reporters.

The locomotive shed at Maes-poeth (4½ m. from Machynlleth), was built to house the three original locomotives on a single road, and was located at the junction of the horse-worked Upper Corris branch, and at the head of the formidable gradient which descended sharply towards Machynlleth at 1 in 35, 1 in 50, 1 in 330 and 1 in 64, all within the ensuing mile of track. 'Up' trains at this location were not helped by having to negotiate some momentum-sapping curves at Pont y Goedwig, at the foot of the final 1 in 35. Indeed, the whole character of the line from Maes-poeth southwards towards Machynlleth was in marked contrast to the more northern section, where the valley, although somewhat less wooded and more bleak, had the appearance of being broader, straighter and more open. To the south of Corris, much the opposite obtains. Here, the little Afon Dulas squeezes through narrow glens, negotiates its way around huge boulders, cascades from pool to pool,

9

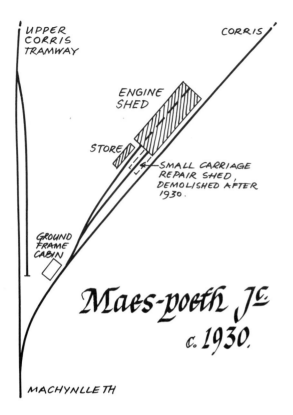

UPPER CORRIS TRAMWAY

CORRIS

ENGINE SHED

STORE

SMALL CARRIAGE REPAIR SHED, DEMOLISHED AFTER 1930.

GROUND FRAME CABIN

Maes-poeth Jᶜ
c. 1930.

MACHYNLLETH

glides by verdant pastures or spills over loose rocks in its strenuous effort to gain the Dyfi near Machynlleth. This section of the valley possesses great charm and variety, alas, frequently unnoticed by the modern traveller who concentrates on the twisting road, steering, braking and accelerating, in a vain attempt to make rapid progress over a route which has been improved but which, thankfully, can never be entirely straightened.

If the line in the Aberllefenni—Maes-poeth sector seemed free to choose its own path through meadows or along the hillside, the southern section from the shed adhered relentlessly to each twist and turn of the adjacent A487, almost as though the railway lacked confidence to strike out on its own.

In truth, of course, the path earlier chosen by the turnpike surveyors, and followed with such fidelity by the Corris, offered the simplest and

most economical route between Maes-poeth and Ffridd Gate and, as a consequence, produced what James Boyd refers to as the Corris's 'impossible curves'. These contributed greatly to the peculiar charm of the line. Narrow-gauge trains, by their very nature, cover the ground only slowly and a journey can become tedious for those who are not particularly enamoured of this mode of travel. This applies particularly if the track is straight, causing the view from the train to remain fairly constant and slow-changing. Such a criticism could hardly be levelled at the Corris, for whatever else its shortcomings, it seemed that hardly a yard of the route between Maes-poeth and Ffridd Gate could be traversed without the train changing direction, resulting in an ever varied kaleidoscope of river and mountain scenery. The experience may still be enjoyed to a degree from the road, of course, and is particularly rewarding during the autumn, but the little trains offered a further advantage which we can no longer enjoy today. The seating in the coaches was so arranged that passengers received the benefit of a broadside view of the valley which, with the leisurely pace of the train, proved most advantageous as the scene changed slowly but constantly, in an engaging manner.

This attractive part of the journey was punctuated by small wayside stations or halts, at Pont Ifans and Esgairgeiliog (3m. 44ch.) and again at Llwyn-gwern (2m. 22ch.) Lliwdy, Doldderwen, and Ffridd Gate. Horse-worked quarry branches joined the line at Esgairgeiliog and Llwyn-gwern and minor roads crossed the main line on the level at Pont Ifans, Llwyn-gwern and Ffridd Gate. The character of the line changed again here, as a result of the gradient which carried it straight down across the Dyfi to the broad meadows beyond. These form part of the Dyfi flood plain and are still subjected regularly to the vagaries of the river.

The final gradient from Ffridd Gate commenced at 1 in 132 for the first furlong or so, steepened to 1 in 37 for about a furlong and a half, and eased to 1 in 50 at the approach to the river bridge before attaining something near level track at the outskirts of Machynlleth.

10

Humphrey and No. 3 pose for J. I. C. Boyd's camera outside Maes-poeth shortly before the closure. The old carriage siding lies buried beneath the debris in the foreground but an indication of its roof-line is just discernible to the right of the main entrance. 1947/8.

LGRP

Few photographs exist of the interior of Maespoeth shed; this portrait of No. 3 undergoing some attention to the motion is particularly successful and, if the paint work is any indication, shows the engine to be in good condition at this time. 5.8.1935.

F. M. Butterfield: courtesy R. C. Riley

Positive identification of the little Falcons in early photographs is often difficult as the number plates were too small to be read with certainty, and no numbers were displayed on the buffer beams. Detail differences were many and varied over the years and the number of accurately dated prints which also show the number of the engine clearly are few and far between. Educated guesses can sometimes prove lucky and although several people have endeavoured to establish a definitive list of detail changes, with dates, the wary know that no sooner does a 'code' seem credible than a 'new' photograph emerges, which effectively destroys the previous theory.

No engine number appears to have been recorded by the photographer but a carfeul note was made of the date. The location could well be the final 1 in 35 on the approach to Maespoeth; the engine is certainly working hard. 10.7.1915.

H. W. Burman, courtesy C. C. Green

Llwyngwern level-crossing. Price Owen and Driver Humphreys appear to be transferring the crossing gate keys as No. 3 takes its train through on 9.7.1948.

GBJ

No. 3 works a very light train through the level-crossing at Pont Ifans. The stone-built gate-keepers shelter, so essential during passenger days, is visible just to the left of the cab. Note the old sack covering the side opening; a keen wind whistling through the cab could be decidedly uncomfortable.

AGW, courtesy R. C. Riley

The Plans & Sections submitted for the 1858 Parliamentary session show that the original intention here was to strike directly across what later became the Newtown & Machynlleth Railway (N & M) goods yard. When it became apparent that construction of that railway would follow hard on the heels of the Corris, it was obviously considered prudent to make a diversion around the site, to the north: the fact that Earl Vane and R. D. Pryce had influence on both Boards must have contributed to the early acceptance of the revised scheme.

Three stables were erected alongside this diversion, and strategically located near the junction of the long incline from the quarries and the much more level three miles or so to the quays at Derwen-las and Morben. By 1862, the N & M presence was strong at Machynlleth and there is evidence, referred to later, that some slabs and slates were sent by the standard gauge in June that year, and fully six months before the N & M was officially opened. On the evidence of the only known contemporary illustration of this site (*Illustrated London News*, Jan. 1863) there were then no sidings in the area later occupied by the lower yard at Machynlleth, so the transfer of any slate traffic would have taken place in the upper yard. The N & M was evidently encouraged by this traffic for an agreement was sealed in 1863, allowing the Corris to enter the N & M yard. As the upper yard was impracticable for all but the pioneer transfers, it would seem that the N & M quickly laid a siding into what later became the lower yard, in order to attract more traffic.

Maps or other diagrams of this era are not available at present. In their absence, it seems reasonable to assume that only a short length of standard-gauge siding was laid initially, and that the Corris would have constructed a spur from their Derwen-las line to serve it.

In later years the wharves were extended and the Corris layout at the site developed into that line's southern terminus for both passenger and freight working.

After diverting around the N & M site *c.* 1859/60, the tramway continued west of Machynlleth by crossing the site later occupied by the Crosville Company, proceeding behind the Baptist Chapel in Heol y Doll (Toll Street), through the area of the town known as the Garsiwn and skirting what later became the playing fields of the County School. The route past Ogo Fach and Nawlyn to Derwen-las, although almost level, remained tortuous as the engineer (Arthur Causton, of Gloucester) sought to keep the line above the flood level. The long embankment constructed in 1862/3 by the Aberystwyth & Welsh Coast Company, between Machynlleth and Glandovey Junction (as it then was), has successfully diverted much of

The photograph of Ffridd Wood, just north of Machynlleth, illustrates well the close proximity of road and rail which existed for the better part of four miles between Ffridd Gate and Maespoeth Junction. The Upper Corris branch, although it left the main line at that point, continued faithfully alongside the turnpike for a further two miles or so. The rails were set between 1 ft and 3 ft lower than the road and followed the latter's alignment religiously, which resulted in an abundance of check-railed curves on this section. The deceptively low wall to the right of the track marks a drop of 15-20 ft to a feeder for the local mill, and the river Dulas, both obscured by the lush foliage. c. 1920.

PPC: GBJ Coll.

This popular view is worthy of inclusion as it portrays clearly the broad concrete and rubble base surrounding each pier of the later Dyfi river bridge. It also demonstrates the relatively direct course of the river above the bridge at this time, whilst those with a keen eye for perspective will appreciate that the bridge did not cross the river on the level but was inclined to meet the 1 in 32 to Ffridd Gate, to the left of the photograph.

The light coloured paintwork on the van was a pink primer on some new woodwork. The van remained on the Corris for this repair and it is most probable that the work was carried out during a weekend, at Maespoeth. Precisely who carried out the repair, however, is not known. c.1945.

Real photographs

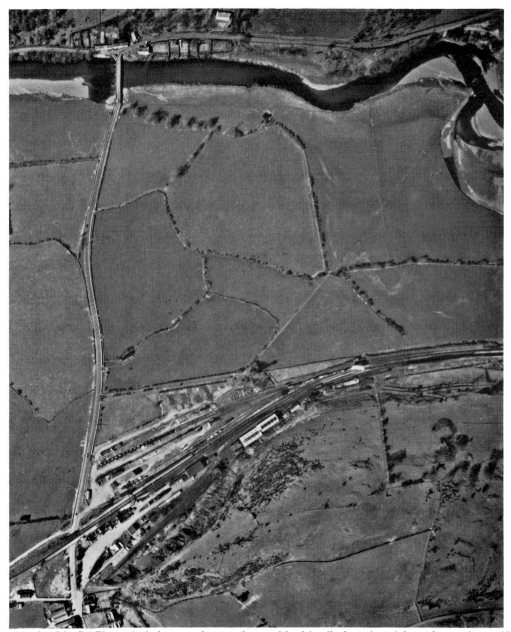

This example of the RAF's vertical photography reveals a wealth of detail when viewed through a good magnifying glass. Taken almost five years after the Corris had closed, evidence of the little line was still visible from the air in 1953. Points of particular interest are the area around the river bridge and the line of the 1859 deviation around the standard gauge yard. 10.4.1953.

Crown Copyright

15

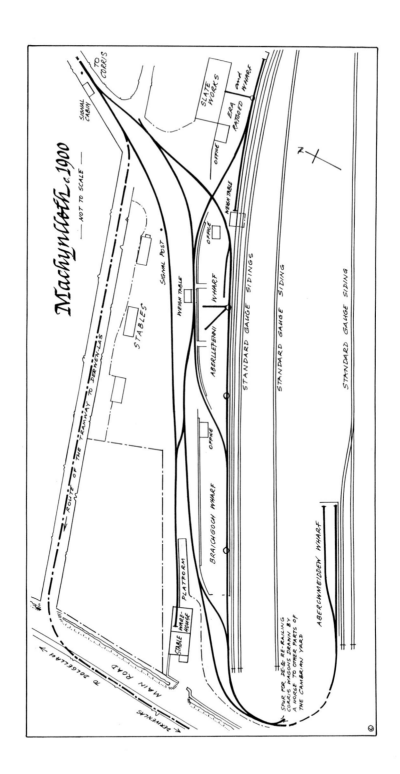

Machynlleth c.1900
— NOT TO SCALE —

TO CORRIS

SIGNAL CABIN

SLATE WORKS

ERA AND WHARF

OFFICE

N

WEIGH TABLE

ROUTE OF THE TRAMWAY TO DERWENLAS

STABLES

SIGNAL POST

WEIGH TABLE

OFFICE

OFFICE

WHARF

ABERLLEFENNI

STANDARD GAUGE SIDINGS

STANDARD GAUGE SIDING

STANDARD GAUGE SIDING

BRAICHGOCH WHARF

ABERCWMEIDDEW WHARF

SPUR FOR DE-&-RE-RAILING CORRIS WAGONS DRAWN BY A HORSE TO OTHER PARTS OF THE CAMBRIAN YARD

PLATFORM

WARE-HOUSE

STABLE

MAIN ROAD

TO DOLGELLAU

DERWENLAS

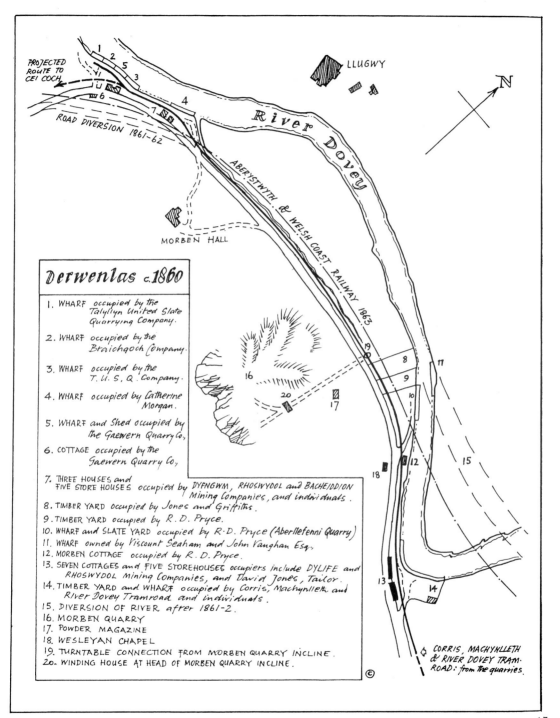

PROJECTED ROUTE TO CEI COCH

LLUGWY

N

ROAD DIVERSION 1861-62

River Dovey

ABERYSTWYTH & WELSH COAST RAILWAY 1863

MORBEN HALL

Derwenlas c.1860

1. WHARF occupied by the Talyllyn United Slate Quarrying Company.
2. WHARF occupied by the Braichgoch Company.
3. WHARF occupied by the T.U.S.Q. Company.
4. WHARF occupied by Catherine Morgan.
5. WHARF and Shed occupied by the Gaewern Quarry Co.
6. COTTAGE occupied by the Gaewern Quarry Co.
7. THREE HOUSES and FIVE STORE HOUSES occupied by DYFNGWM, RHOSWYDOL and BACHEIDDION Mining Companies, and individuals.
8. TIMBER YARD occupied by Jones and Griffiths.
9. TIMBER YARD occupied by R.D. Pryce.
10. WHARF and SLATE YARD occupied by R.D. Pryce (Aberllefenni Quarry)
11. WHARF owned by Viscount Seaham and John Vaughan Esq.
12. MORBEN COTTAGE occupied by R.D. Pryce.
13. SEVEN COTTAGES and FIVE STOREHOUSES occupiers include DYLIFE and RHOSWYDOL Mining Companies, and David Jones, Tailor.
14. TIMBER YARD and WHARF occupied by Corris, Machynlleth and River Dovey Tramroad and individuals.
15. DIVERSION OF RIVER after 1861-2.
16. MORBEN QUARRY
17. POWDER MAGAZINE
18. WESLEYAN CHAPEL
19. TURNTABLE CONNECTION FROM MORBEN QUARRY INCLINE.
20. WINDING HOUSE AT HEAD OF MORBEN QUARRY INCLINE.

Ⓒ

CORRIS, MACHYNLLETH & RIVER DOVEY TRAMROAD: from the quarries.

the flooding away from the Garsiwn area of the town. This embankment was breached by the tramway which used a single masonry arch alongside the main Dolgellau/Tywyn road, just below the Cambrian station. This remains, although it is now bricked-up.

Information concerning arrangements at Derwen-las and Morben is sparse, and much of what is available is both intriguing and nebulous! The Plans & Sections for 1858 show that a branch was proposed from the main tramway to the west of the wharves, to the river below Llyn y Bwtri, whilst the tramway was to continue to Cei Coch at Garreg, below Glandyfi Castle. The early appearance of the standard-gauge railway rendered this final extension (and probably the branch) unnecessary and it is extremely doubtful whether this latter section was constructed. As it was, the Machynlleth —Morben section of the tramway saw extensive use only from 1859 to 1863. Thereafter, the output of the quarries was increasingly diverted to the standard gauge at Machynlleth, although the tramway still saw some use throughout the 1860s and was not finally abandoned and lifted until the following decade.

The formative years: 1858-1878

The opening of the Newtown & Machynlleth Railway[3] undoubtedly encouraged the quarry owners to transfer their products directly to the standard gauge at Machynlleth at the earliest opportunity and at a local meeting of the N & M Board on 2 July 1863, an agreement was quickly sealed permitting the Corris Tramroad to convey slates into the Machynlleth yard.[4] It would appear, therefore, that the first wharf, possibly the section later used exclusively by the Aberllefenni Company, dates from this period.

The N & M became one of the original constituent companies which formed the Cambrian Railways in 1864, and within two years of its inception the new Cambrian Board was approached (in May 1866) for an additional wharf at Machynlleth—'for the Braichgoch and others'—which was stated to be 'much wanted' and estimated to cost £85. Whether this work was immediately

carried out is not apparent but, just over three years later, on 7 June 1869, the Cambrian Engineer again approached his Board with a similar request:

> Some additional wharfage accommodation is required at Machynlleth for the above quarries (Braichgoch and others) and this may be easily obtained by extending the siding in the lower yard, which may be done with some old rails and building some low walls to wharves.[5]

The cost of the work this time was estimated at £60 and its necessity suggests either the inadequacy of the 1866 extension or, possibly, that the wharf had not then been constructed, although it seems unlikely that a facility which would have promoted additional freight traffic—all too sparse on the Cambrian—could have been deferred for three years.

Early Passenger arrangements

The Corris tramway was constructed for the conveyance of slates but it seems that passengers were also transported from the outset, unofficially perhaps, but on a fairly regular basis nonetheless (see Appendix I). Such circumstances hardly pleased the quarry owners who maintained that the tramway was for their exclusive use. By the mid 1870s, however, active steps were taken to establish an official passenger service and to take advantage of the powers of an earlier Act of 1864 sanctioning the use of steam locomotives.

On 6 October 1874, the Secretary of the Corris Company, James Fraser, wrote from the Company's offices at 7 Bank Buildings, London EC, to George Owen, the Cambrian's Engineer, again seeking land at Machynlleth to expand their operation:

> We have been carting passengers and goods up from Machynlleth to Corris and it is astonishing what a number will go up if we had any sufficient accommodation [sic]. As a beginning we would like to build a little warehouse and stable at Machynlleth and I am told that your Company may be willing to let us have space at their yard for this purpose . . .[6]

Machynlleth yard, looking north-east. The main line curves away on the left, whilst the siding on the extreme right leads to the Aberllefenni wharf. The centre line, which shows some evidence of sanding, formed part of the goods loop. The tall disc, indicating the position of the adjacent trap point, together with the signal and box, were removed in 1940. The corrugated zinc and slate buildings on the old Ratgoed/ERA wharf (right) were also demolished around that time. The original Derwenlas tramway would have curved very sharply to the left of the picture, into the lane just indicated by the presence of the two check rails in the middle distance, this side of the signal box. c.1932.

Real Photographs

Machynlleth yard, looking east. The Derwenlas route followed the hedgegrow in the middle distance, to the left; one of the three stables originally at this site stood just to the left of the signal. The Ratgoed/ERA enamelling shed is visible in the centre distance whilst the small shuttered building in the foreground housed the narrow gauge weigh machine—the table itself is just visible on the extreme right. The dense shadow hereabouts is created by the rear face of the Aberllefenni wharf, whose advertising name-board is prominent, whilst the small shed just beyond served as an office-cum-mess room. 12.8.1935.

H. F. Wheeler, courtesy R. S. Carpenter

19

The matter was not resolved promptly as the two parties did not immediately agree on the site required by the Corris. The initial request seemed straightforward but the Cambrian responded by suggesting two sites, both unsuitable and fraught with practical difficulties. The first option, near the turnpike, lacked standard-gauge facilities, (even supposing the Derwen-las tramway extension remained *in situ*), whilst the second alternative would have called for a tramway extension into the Cambrian's upper yard, involving crossing the main line and gaining a height of approximately 20ft. George Owen replied:

> . . . my Board . . . have every desire to accommodate you but the difficulty is what you require. We have some land on the south west side of the turn-pike road that would I think suit you, or we might manage to put you in the upper yard but any erections you might have to put up would have to be taken down on a short notice to that effect, if we should require the site upon which they have been placed.[7]

The principal difficulty, however, appeared merely to be poor communication, a fact well appreciated by David Owen, the Corris Manager at this time, and demonstrated in his letter of 9 November to Fraser,

> If Mr George Owen would make it convenient to come down to [meet] me on the spot someday, I believe the matter could be settled in a few minutes.[8]

Indeed, such was the case, but it was not until April 1875 that the Cambrian Engineer was in a position to report:

> I have met their manager at Machynlleth . . . we have found that the only suitable place was at 'A' on the accompanying plan. The warehouse is required for the storage of grain, flour and other goods from the Cambrian destined for Corris, and the stable is required for feeding at mid day the two horses that work the passenger trains to and from the quarries, but these horses are stabled at the other end at night.[9]

By the end of the following month, George Owen was reporting to his Board again that he had 'prepared a plan of the above yard showing the exact points of the Corris Railway, both at the present period and at the time of the construction of your railway'. Most regrettably, neither of these early plans appears to have survived, making it difficult at this date to be precise regarding the building sequence of the wharves, buildings and various sidings.

Thus evolved the station layout at Machynlleth. Whilst a definitive early map may not be available at present, various references such as the foregoing provide a series of clues which, although lacking the authenticity of a diagram, enable us to gain some idea of the pattern of early developments.

It seems clear, however, that the final wharf constructed especially for slate transhipment at Machynlleth was built for the Abercwmeiddew Quarry[10] *c.* 1877-8. By that time, all the tramway land adjacent to the standard gauge was occupied, so the Abercwmeiddew facility had to be constructed further across the Cambrian yard, requiring an extension of the tramway. When the request was considered in March 1877, the estimated cost of the new 100ft × 25ft wharf was put at £87.2s.0d. and the cost of the tramway extension, 'which should be defrayed by the quarry proprietors', amounted to £42.0s.0d.[11]

Whilst this may have been the last request for an additional wharf, business was obviously expanding during this period and by September 1878 the Cambrian Board was in receipt of yet another request from the Corris seeking, this time, to install a loop line to facilitate the new locomotive operation, shortly to be introduced. Owen reported,

> This work cannot be carried out without removing the fence forming the boundary of a field belonging to your Company, back some six feet. The land required . . . will be 64 yards . . . I would recommend the removal of the fence.[12]

That the Corris was a progressive and successful company at this time is borne out by the fact that it caught the attention of the Imperial Tramways Company of Bristol and was, in fact, taken over by

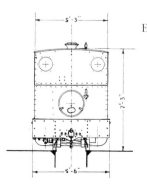

A Cambrian Railways telegraph message relayed from Pritchard, the Cambrian Agent at Dolgellau, to J. R. Dix in his capacity as the Cambrian Agent at Machynlleth, in 1876, before he joined the Corris as General Manager.

GBJ Collection

them during 1878: from 1887, this company was known as the Bristol Tramways & Carriage Company Limited. Precisely how a Bristol company became attracted to a narrow-gauge quarry line in mid Wales has yet to be fully explained, but the Corris was obviously a sound investment, and remained so, for over three decades.

Some improvements were already in hand at the time of the take-over but it would appear that the major impetus for up-grading the track, rolling stock and motive power was provided by the Bristol company, which also appointed a new manager before the year was out.

The régime of J. R. Dix: 1878-1907

The appointment of Mr J. R. Dix, a former Cambrian Railways Traffic Manager at Machynlleth, became effective from 3 December 1878; he was an energetic administrator and proved an inspired choice. In addition to being an able and experienced railwayman, Dix undoubtedly revealed something of a Midas touch as far as the Corris was concerned, although it should be borne in mind that the seeds of his ideas were sown during the fertile period when the horse presented the only real alternative to the railway system.

By the end of 1878, the Hughes Locomotive and Tramway Engine Company, of the Falcon Works, Loughborough, had delivered three 0-4-0 saddle-tank locomotives for the new service, together with some four-wheel carriages. The latter had open, verandah ends and were reminiscent of street tramcars; the first-class cars boasted cushions covered with green plush, which must have represented a considerable improvement over previous vehicles used by passengers.[13]

Engine No. 3

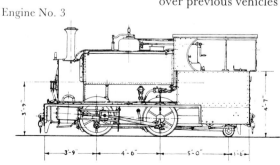
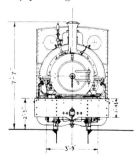

The new, rather tram-like, carriages delivered in 1878 were initially drawn by two horses and represented a considerable advance on the previous (and quite unofficial) vehicles. However, when horse-power was replaced by steam from 1883, the deficiencies of the short wheel-base were emphasised, resulting in the development of a new design. The first bogie carriage thus arrived in 1888 and a process of adapting the existing stock, by mounting two of the original bodies on a new bogie underframe, had eliminated all the old four-wheel carriages within five years.

This photograph of four-wheel First Class carriage No. 8 was taken at Corris, soon after its arrival. The roofs of two of these vehicles, made redundant as a result of the conversions to bogie coaches, served side by side as a hay loft above the stalls in one of the stables at Machynlleth until the stable was demolished c. 1948.

Anon: GBJ Coll.

Nonetheless, the quarry owners remained unhappy about the conveyance of passengers, maintaining that they interfered with the efficient despatch of slate. As a result, passenger services were withdrawn. Several challenges thus awaited the new manager; he had to placate the quarry owners and he had also to meet the additional statutory requirements as a result of up-grading the line, which called for a new Act of Parliament. Success did not come immediately but Dix achieved both objectives in due course and as soon as the Act was obtained, steam-hauled passenger services commenced at once between Machynlleth and

Corris, on 4 July 1883. These were extended to Aberllefenni in 1887.

The years of Dix's management, undeniably, were prosperous times and represent the Golden Age of the Corris. Despite the fluctuating fortunes experienced by various quarries during this period he guided the railway's finances with a sure hand, resulting in dividends of up to 8%.[14]

The early years of the new century, however, were to witness many changes and the variable circumstances and fortunes of the slate industry eventually began to have an adverse effect on the finances of the railway. The latter managed to

CORRIS RAILWAY.

Cheap Return Tickets

WILL BE ISSUED FROM

MAY 1st to OCTOBER 31st, 1894, from

CORRIS

TO

ABERYSTWYTH,

BORTH, ABERDOVEY,

Towyn, Barmouth,

AND

DOLGELLEY,

AS FOLLOWS:—

CORRIS TO	DAY TRIP TICKETS. Issued Daily. Returning on day of issue.		Week end TICKETS. Issued on Fridays or Saturdays, Returning on Monday or Tuesday following.	
	1st Class.	3rd Class.	1st Class.	3rd Class.
Aberystwyth -	3s. 6d.	2s. 0d.	5s.	3s.
Borth - - -	2s. 6d.	1s. 6d.	4s.	2s. 6d.
Aberdovey - -	2s. 6d.	1s. 6d.	4s.	2s. 3d.
Towyn - - -	3s. 0d.	1s. 9d.	4s. 6d.	2s. 9d.
Barmouth - -	4s. 6d.	2s. 6d.	6s.	3s. 6d.
Dolgelley - -	5s. 6d.	3s. 0d.	6s.	3s. 6d.

Available by any of the Ordinary Trains.

J. R. DIX,

GENERAL MANAGER.

Corris, May 1st, 1894.

JOHN WHITRIDGE, "COLUMBIAN" PRINTING WORKS, OSWESTRY.

Printer's Proof of the new poster for 1894 amended, more than likely, by Mr. Dix himself.

GBJ Coll.

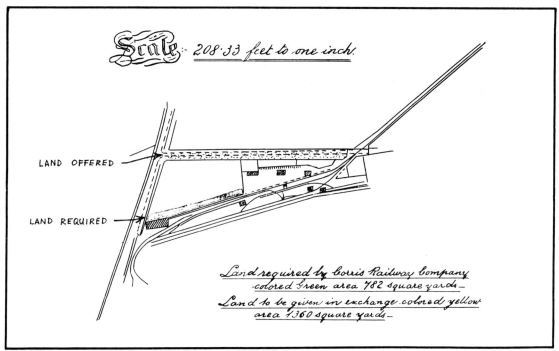

Scale:- 208.33 feet to one inch.

LAND OFFERED

LAND REQUIRED

Land required by Corris Railway Company
- colored Green area 782 square yards-
Land to be given in exchange colored yellow
area 1360 square yards-

This plan, doubtless produced by the versatile Mr. Dix before the station at Machynlleth was re-built in 1906, is not entirely accurate but indicates the general layout at the turn of the Century.

GBJ Coll.

maintain a confident facade by undertaking the rebuilding of Machynlleth station in 1904, and by constructing a new steel-girder bridge across the Dyfi in 1906, but the returns for that year also revealed a working loss for the first time during Dix's period as Manager. The railway's greatest loss at this time, however, was the dismissal of Dix himself. It evolved when the Directors discovered that he was a partner in a private company which sold coal to the railway. That previous Directors had sanctioned such an action in 1880 was discounted; Dix was not re-instated and his departure, in June 1907, marked the beginning of a period of decline for the Corris that was to continue slowly but steadily for the remainder of its existence.

O'Sullivan's term of office: 1907-1917

Although Dix's successor, Mr J. J. O'Sullivan, entered office at a difficult time, he was an exper-ienced man, having recently retired from the post of Manager of the Cork, Blackrock & Passage Railway. He was related to Sir J. Clifton Robinson, the Managing Director, and was also a business associate of Sir George White, Chairman of Bristol Tramways. In some respects he faced greater difficulties than his predecessor and it is to his credit that he was able to demonstrate managerial skills which generally matched those of Dix. O'Sullivan's greatest concern at the outset must have been the serious loss of traffic resulting from the closure of two of the largest quarries in the district, both, as it happened, on the Upper Corris branch: Abercwmeiddew had closed in 1904, followed later by the large and influential Braich-goch Company, forced to cease operation in 1906. Although these events had occurred at the end of Dix's tenure, the loss of revenue on this scale was

24

Although then still in operation, the Braichgoch quarry presented a sad picture of decline by the 1960s. It had severed connection with the Corris line in 1926 but the path of the tramway onwards to the Upper Corris quarries may be seen on the extreme left of the picture as it curved behind the main office block and manager's accommodation. Access from this branch was provided from a point behind the camera and the path of the line into the main yard may be discerned in the centre of the picture. The few rows of stacked slates at this point are a miserable reminder of the vast stocks which were held in the yard in the past. June 1960.

WIMM

A view of part of Braichgoch quarry, taken from the top of the incline shown in the centre of the previous photograph, showing (top right) the old and narrow Corris-Dolgellau road with, just below it, the route of the Upper Corris branch. Two adits are discernible burrowing into the mountainside beneath tramway and road, one beneath the parapet on the side of the tramway, at the top of the picture, and the second adjacent to the corrugated-iron roof at lower right. A ballast wagon, used for balancing loads on the incline on which the photographer stood, is just visible on the bottom edge of the original print. 1974.

R. W. Kidner

CAMBRIAN & CORRIS RAILWAYS.

Talyllyn Lake, Cader Idris, The Corris Valley, and Dolycae Waterfall.

CHEAP RETURN TICKETS

WILL BE ISSUED TO

TAL·Y·LLYN

DAILY (Sundays excepted), from July 1st, to September 30th, 1897.

FROM	Times of Departure		Fares for the Double Journey, including Rail and Coach.	
			1st.	3rd.
	a.m.	p.m.	s. d.	s. d.
ABERYSTWYTH	8 30 or	12 30	5 3	3 9
BOW STREET	8 40 „	12 40	4 9	3 6
LLANFIHANGEL	8 44 „	12 44	4 9	3 6
BORTH	8 48 „	12 49	4 3	3 3
GLANDOVEY	9 3 „	1 3	3 9	2 9
ABERDOVEY	8 35 „	12 18	4 3	3 3
TOWYN	8 24 „	12 6	4 9	3 6
DOLGELLEY	7 35 „	11 0	7 3	4 9
BARMOUTH	7 50 „	11 35	6 3	4 3
MACHYNLLETH (Corris Railway)	9 30 „	1 30	3 3	2 6

☞ Excursionists by this Trip travel by rail to Corris (changing at Machynlleth into the Miniature Gauge train). Leave Corris by Coach at 10·0 a.m. or 2·0 p.m., and arrive at Talyllyn Lake at 10·45 a.m. or 2·45 p.m. Leave Talyllyn Lake at 11·15 a.m. or 4·15 p.m. by Road Conveyance for Corris, proceeding from Corris by the Miniature Gauge Railway at 12·25 or 5·25 p.m. to Machynlleth.

"Throughout the journey there is one everchanging panorama of rugged rock, pine-clothed hill, snowy waterfall, rushing streams, green woods, and cultivated fields."—"Montgomery County Times."

"No one sojourning here even for a few days should fail to visit Corris, Talyllyn Lake, and Cader Idris."—"Cardigan Bay Visitor."

For further particulars apply to the Station Masters, or the Enquiry Offices at
ABERYSTWYTH.—Messrs. Wheatley & Sons, Music Warehouse, Terrace Road.
          Mr. H. H. Davies, Photographer, Pier Street.
BARMOUTH—Mr. John Evans, Stationer, Glanymor House.
    „   Mr. Hugh Davies, Chemist, St. Ann's Square.
BARMOUTH & DOLGELLEY—Mrs. Arnfield, Music Warehouse.
DOLGELLEY, TOWYN & ABERDOVEY—Mr. O. H. Young, Photographer.

Corris: Printed by the "Idris" Press Company.

a cause of great concern which handicapped O'Sullivan considerably.

The rough draft of a report to Sir Clifton Robinson on the state of quarrying in the district has survived, and makes interesting reading (Appendix II).

O'Sullivan was fortunate, however, that the changeable and unsettled nature of the slate traffic was countered to some extent by the bourgeoning tourist trade, as increasing numbers of summer visitors were persuaded to frequent the seaside resorts of Cardigan Bay. Many were attracted inland on day excursions, to sample the delights of mountain scenery, and one of the most popular packages was the circular tour run in conjunction with the Cambrian and Tal-y-llyn Railways. In 1907, O'Sullivan sought to link the two narrow-gauge lines by an extension from Upper Corris, utilising electric traction, but the proposal came to nought. The circular tours, however, became established favourites, with the connection between Corris and Tal-y-llyn provided initially by the Corris Railway's horse-drawn wagonettes. These were later replaced by new motor charabancs, the first of which appeared in 1908, delivered, predictably, from Bristol. [15]

Although it posed no serious threat at the outset of his term of office, O'Sullivan had increasingly to contend with the new phenomenon of road transport; indeed, such were its attractions that he gradually increased the operation of railway-owned road motors, a policy which was continued by his successor.

Slate traffic was maintained at a reasonable level during the period leading to the Great War. Aberllefenni Quarry's tonnage by rail—3,689 tons in 1909—reached 4,251 tons by 1913, although Llwyn-gwern Quarry (649 tons in 1909) did not fare as well, being forced to close in 1911. However, by 1913, the New Rhiwgwreiddyn and New ERA quarries, near Esgairgeiliog, had started modest production (234 tons and 621 tons, respectively), and Abercwmeiddew re-opened, producing a moderate 388 tons. Although the Braich-goch

Machynlleth station, 1910, just a few years after completing the rebuilding of the station and new loop. The ground covering consists of small pieces of quarry waste but it is still fairly stoney and fresh at this time, in contrast to later years when it was generally ground down to a finer, more powdery grade. The low boundary wall at the edge of the loop also appears in good order, as might be anticipated at this time. 1910.

P. B. Chatwin Coll. courtesy C. C. Green

Quarry remained officially closed during this period, some wagon loads of building stone left periodically over the Upper Corris branch, for Machynlleth. [16]

If the onset of the First World War affected the tourist figures adversely, some compensation was provided by the dramatic increase in demand for home-grown timber. Several Welsh narrow-gauge lines were to benefit from timber traffic and the Corris converted many wagons by locating bolsters directly on the wagon frames. Timber traffic must have been quite considerable and a temporary branch was laid from Lliwdy along the road to Esgair, specifically for this purpose. Branches were also extended into the forestry at Esgair-geiliog and Matthew's Mill. Although this traffic did not survive much into the 30s, it certainly appeared to have continued throughout the 1920s, for the Rolling Stock returns for June 1930 listed no fewer than 17 timber wagons.

Post war optimism: D. J. McCourt at the helm

In 1917, J. J. O'Sullivan died suddenly at the age of 68, whilst still in office. He was at work in Corris one Friday in April but felt unwell on returning to his home at Aberystwyth, and died the next day. Following his death, F. W. Withers, of the Bristol company acted as General Manager and Secretary. It appears he had little contact with the area but merely kept matters in order until the appointment of Mr D. J. McCourt in 1921.

By the end of the war, the Abercwmeiddew tonnage by rail had dwindled again. The last

An old winding house stands at the head of an incline, a silent monument to a forgotten industry. It marks a spot on the bleak hillside which was once a location of much activity and industry, as loaded wagons were manoeuvred into position beneath the large drum, under the roof, and lowered to the level below. The descent was regulated by the lever located inside the right-hand wall, which was connected to a large brake-shoe acting directly on the drum. The location is believed to be at Abercwmeiddew quarry, which has been much changed and landscaped in recent years. September 1970.

R. W. Kidner

outward traffic (103 tons) featured in the 1922 accounts and although a handful of men continued to work at the quarry until the outbreak of the Second World War, no further traffic went by narrow gauge. The fortunes of the Braich-goch, on the other hand, took a decided turn for the better; it re-opened in 1919, the modest tonnage of 159 for that year leaping substantially to 1,058 tons in 1920 and 1,045 tons in 1921.

Even Llwyn-gwern re-opened in 1920, with a limited output by rail of 171 tons, but by 1925 the figure was no better than 126 tons; the final entry for Llwyn-gwern in the accounts is a miserable 7 cwt in 1928. It is doubtful whether the quarry traffic of the 1920s used the timber and stone viaduct at this location, for this is reported to have collapsed *c.* 1909 and such small tonnages could as easily have been carted directly to the nearby siding, which remained open at least until November 1930. A revealing memorandum sent to Machynlleth Low Level station from the Oswestry Traffic Manager's Office (5.9.1930) enquired:

> In view of the fact that the Llwyngwern siding has not been used since 1909, do you see any reason why the facility should not be taken up?

The reply, dispatched the following day, must have stated that the siding, or at least that part of it on the railway side of the viaduct, was still in use, for another letter of 8 September opens:

> I am obliged for your letter of the 6th inst. and shall be glad if you will please let me have particulars of

the traffic dealt with at Llwyngwern siding during the last month.

This traffic comprised 2 cwt of sugar on the 14th; 1½ tons of grain grounds on the 20th (to Ratgoed), and 4 cwt of grain on the 27th.[17] Llwyn-gwern quarry continued in operation until the early 1950s but the siding was not *in situ* at the close; it was probably removed during the scrap drive of 1940/1.

The traffic emanating from Aberllefenni, for so long the mainstay of Corris fortunes, also declined between 1902 and 1918 (from 5,185 tons to 1,809 tons), but the optimism of the post-war period saw a recovery to 2,909 tons by 1920 and 3,196 tons by 1923. These more heartening figures were noted by the Bristol Board which was encouraged to reinforce the locomotive stock by ordering a new engine, for the three original locomotives were all by this time over forty years old. The first thought was for another product of the Falcon Works, as the Hughes design was well suited to the needs of the Corris. A direct re-order was not possible, however, as neither the original company nor design were available. A compromise, in the form of a Kerr Stuart 0-4-2ST design, was finally chosen. It never fully matched its older stablemates, either in terms of efficiency or popularity, although it possessed greater headroom in the cab and was equipped with sanding gear, two useful features lacking on the little Falcons.

Just as Corris fortunes appeared to recover after the Great War, they suffered a second blow at the hands of Braich-goch, when the railway introduced

Engine No. 4

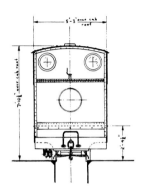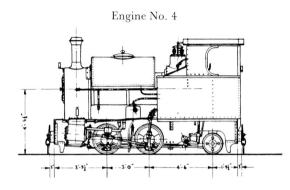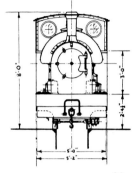

new rates from 1 July 1925[18]. This obviously displeased Braich-goch a great deal, for the quarry immediately countered the move by purchasing a steam lorry and transferring a substantial portion of its output to road. The figure of 1,860 tons by rail for 1925 was reduced to 1,123 tons in 1926 and a year later it had fallen dramatically to 118 tons. This was the last occasion for Braich-goch to feature in the Corris Acounts.[19]

On the credit side, it must be stated that the old Cymerau Quarry, on the Ratgoed branch, was re-opened by Inigo Jones in 1922. The average annual tonnage for the ensuing seven years was only a modest 211 tons but the output, mainly slab, was of excellent quality and production continued steadily if not dramatically. This traffic, modest as it was, made an invaluable contribution to the survival of the line, for the quarry continued to function beyond the demise of the railway, until the early 1950s.

As the 1920s progressed, D. J. McCourt continued the road motor policy instigated by O'Sullivan. The bus services were based at Machynlleth, in what must have been a somewhat uneasy partnership with the trains for they competed for space on the restricted station site. During the final years of that decade, the buses even conveyed the Mail between Corris and Machynlleth; the 'up' service, for example, left on the 07.00 hrs bus from Machynlleth Post Office each weekday.

Nonetheless, recognition of the advantages of the buses, first by O'Sullivan and later by McCourt, revealed clearly that it was to the company's advantage to control the new, rival form of transport. Indeed, it was the Road Motor division of the Corris Railway which eventually proved most attractive to the Great Western.

As the end of the decade approached, the Corris staff totalled 33, approximately a third of whom operated the bus service (Appendix IV.ii).

The inn at Braichgoch is situated where the minor road to Aberllefenni leaves the main Dolgellau route by crossing the Upper Corris tramway, on the right of the picture. Although this section was laid only with bridge rail and worked by horses, the standard of the track seems remarkably high, as, indeed, it needed to be with loaded 'runs' on the down journey frequently attaining some respectable speeds. The figure holding the bicycle, the status symbol of the age, might well be one of the fraternity who took great delight in racing the train between Corris and Machynlleth. Victory, accompanied by cries of 'Bike in first!' was, apparently, more common in the 'down' direction than on the upward run! c.1915.

WHS Kingsway Series

When a new engine was required in 1920, the choice fell to Driver William Roberts (left) whose experience on Corris footplates extended back to 1887. His first thoughts were of an up-dated Falcon design but as the original company no longer existed, this was clearly not possible. The alternative closest to his requirement seemed to be the Kerr Stuart Company's 0-4-2ST design and, in consequence, their No. 4047 appeared on the Corris in 1921. It carried this number on its builder's plate until taken over by the Great Western in 1930, although it was referred to as No. 4 from the outset.

Although to a more modern design than the little Falcons, No. 4 was in many ways a more basic machine. It was built to withstand indifferent care and maintenance, as it might have experienced in colonial or industrial use, whilst the Loughborough engines on the other hand, with their more sophisticated valve gear for example, were much finer machines.

During its early days on the Corris, No. 4 developed a cracked chimney, necessitating a temporary and unsightly repair, which remained until the engine received a heavy overhaul at Maespoeth during the autumn of 1928 and winter 1929. c.1923.

J. P. Richards

Composite bogie carriage No. 1, sandwiched between a bus and the mail wagon, in the siding off the loop at Machynlleth. The large stone near the points was just the right length to wedge beneath the lever; in the absence of a porter or guard, it served to keep the points open to allow the engine to run around its train. No Date.

G. H. W. Clifford, courtesy C. C. Green

Buses ruled the roost at Machynlleth Low Level for the four years following the GW take-over. This view depicts the 1906 station building on the right and the rather curious stone-based, wood-framed and zinc clad building in the centre of the picture, which was obviously used as a bus garage but was also considered as a locomotive shed at this time. Sadly none of the three buses are fully visible nor identified, but with the help of one's imagination, it is possible to visualise their royal blue and cream livery. 29.6.1932.

S. W. Baker

Corris Railway Motor Services.

Programme of
CHEAP RETURN TICKETS
AND
COMBINED MOTOR TOURS

From CORRIS AND MACHYNLLETH,

Every Week-day from July 19th, 1926

(CHILDREN HALF-FARE IN EVERY CASE).

Corris to Talyllyn Lake, 2/- Return.   Machynlleth dep. 11.25 a.m. & 2 p.m.
Machynlleth to Talyllyn Lake, 2/10 Return.   Talyllyn Lake dep. 4 p.m.
Machynlleth to Dolgelley, 3/4 Return.   For times see Dolgelley Motor Service
Corris to Dolgelley, 2/6 Return.   Time Table.

**CIRCULAR TOUR to Corris, Talyllyn Lake, Dolgelley,
returning via Penmaenpool, Arthog, Llwyngwril,
Towyn and Aberdovey. Fifty-one miles of the finest
scenery in Wales. Three quarters of an hour
interval at Dolgelley and half-an-hour at Towyn.**

Machynlleth dep. 11.25 a.m.   Return 5.45 p.m.   **4/3 Through Fare**
Corris dep. 12.30 p.m.   Return 6.30 p.m.   **from Corris & Machnlleth.**

Corris to Dinas Mawddwy, 3/- Return (any connecting times).
Machynlleth to Dinas Mawddwy, 2/6 Return (any Bus).
Corris to Llyfnant Valley, 1/2 Return (any connecting times).
Corris to Aberystwyth, 3/6 Return.
Corris to Towyn, 3/- Return.
Corris to Aberdovey, 2/4 Return.
Machynlleth to Aberdovey, 1/10 Return.
Corris to Pennal, 1/6 Return.

Corris to Barmouth, 3/6 Return.   Machynlleth dep. 9.15 a.m.
Machynlleth to Barmouth, 4/4 Return.   and 11.25 a.m.
Corris dep. 9.45 a.m. and 12.30 p.m.
Barmouth dep. 12.30 and 4.00 p.m.
Corris dep. 9.20 p.m.
Machynlleth arr. 9.40 p.m.

Machynlleth to Trawsfynydd, 4/10 Return.   Machynlleth dep. 9.15 a.m.
Machynlleth to Blaenau Festiniog, 6/4 Return.   and 11.25 a.m.
Corris to Trawsfynydd, 4/- Return.   Corris dep. 9.45 a.m. and 12.30 p.m.
Corris to Blaenau Festiniog, 5/8 Return.   Trawsfynydd arr. 12.40 p.m. and 3.35 p.m.
Blaenau Festiniog arr. 1.35 p.m. and 4.30 p.m.
Blaenau Festiniog dep. 5.45 p.m.
Trawsfynydd dep. 5.30 p.m.
Corris arr. 9.20 p.m.
Machynlleth arr. 9.40 p.m.

Machynlleth to Bala, 5/8 Return.   Machynlleth dep. 11.25 a.m.
Corris to Bala, 4/10 Return.   Corris dep. 12.30 p.m.
Bala arr. 4.20 p.m. Bala dep. 5.45
Corris arr. ... Machynlleth ... m.

Corris to Aberhosan, 2/4 Return.   Wednesdays and Stock Sale days
Machynlleth to Aberhosan   Corris dep. 10 a.m. and 4.55 p.m.
1/6 Return.   Aberhosan arr. 11 a.m. and 6 p.m.
Aberhosan dep. 11.15 a.m. and 6.15 p.m.
Corris arr. 7.30 p.m.
Machynlleth dep. 10.30 a.m. and 5.30 p.m.

The issuing of through tickets is subject to the conditions and regulations referred to in the time tables, bills, and notices of the respective Companies on whose railway or coaches they are available, and the holder by accepting a through ticket, agrees that the respective Companies are not to be liable for any loss or damage, injury, delay, or detention, caused or arising off their respective railways or coaches. The contract and liability of each Company are limited to its own railway or vehicles.
Should the ticket be used for any other station than those named upon it, or by and other train, than as above specified, it will be rendered void, and therefore the Fare paid will be liable to forfeiture, and the full Ordinary Fare will become chargeable. The tickets are not transferable. Return Tickets 2/6 and over available 16 days.
For further information respecting the arrangements shown in this bill, application should be made at the Station, or Bus, or to

Machynlleth, July, 1926.   **D. J. McCOURT, General Manager Corris Railway.**

EVAN JONES, PRINTER, MACHYNLLETH.

A comprehensive 1926 Hand-bill advertising a circular
tour via Dolgellau.

GBJ Coll.

Chapter 1: Notes & References

[1] G. Briwnant-Jones (1991) *Railway Through Talerddig*, Gomer Press, pp. 67-72.

[2] Avon-Anglia, Corris Railway Society, p. 16.

[3] 'A truckload of Flags and slates from Machynlleth by rail, the first load that ever came (by rail)'. Kinsey D. (1838-93) Scrap-album/diary. NLW.

Kinsey dates this entry under 22 June 1862. It is possible, or even most probable, therefore, that other loads of slates for more distant locations could also have gone by N & M from this time, despite the fact that the N & M did not open officially until 3 January 1863. Some traffic continued along the Derwen-las tramway for several more years.

[4] Public Record Office (PRO), Kew. File: *RAIL* 517/1.

[5] *RAIL* 92/19.

[6] *RAIL* 92/24.

[7] ibid.

[8] ibid.

[9] *RAIL* 92/25.

[10] Abercwmeiddew was frequently mis-spelt, even by the quarry company itself, although the origins of the word are straightforward, viz. *Aber* = confluence or stream (in this context), *cwm* = valley, *eiddew* = ivy.

[11] *RAIL* 92/27.

[12] *RAIL* 92/28.

[13] Little is known of earlier vehicles used by passengers, other than a general description in an 1878 *Cambrian News*, that they were 'rickety, suffocating and dark boxes'. Corris Railway Society (1988) *A Return to Corris*, Avon-Anglia Publications, p. 17.

[14] Lewis Cozens (1949) *The Corris Railway,* published by the Author. (1992) Re-printed by Corris Railway Society, p. 17.

[15] ibid.

[16] GBJ Collection.

[17] ibid.

[18] ibid.

[19] ibid.

Chapter 2

The Unwanted Gift

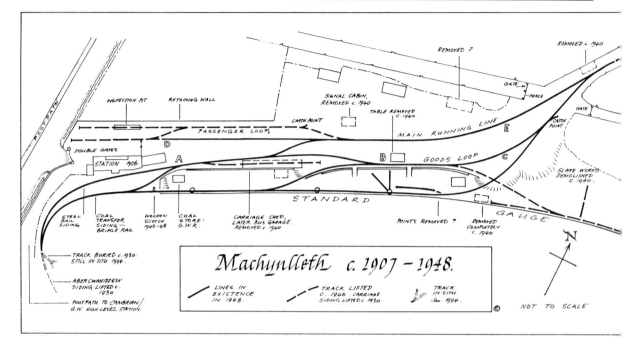

Machynlleth c. 1907 – 1948.

Enter the Great Western: 1930—1948

The most important development to affect the Corris in the 1920s, however, was not based on the economic state of the quarries or, indeed, on any local events, but arose from the death, in 1928, of Sir George White, who owned a controlling interest in the Bristol Tramways Company.

Although the Cambrian had briefly shown interest in leasing the Corris in 1894, and an outright sale to the GWR was considered two years later, both proposals had failed. Even the grouping of 1922/3 disregarded the Corris and the line was left in peace until Sir William McLintock, acting on behalf of the Trustees in February 1929, offered to dispose of Sir George's interests to the GWR. As these were centred mainly in and around the City of Bristol, the Great Western sought, amongst other proposals:

i) [To make] Immediate approach ... to the Bristol Corporation in respect of trams and buses within the City area, in order to ascertain if they desire to purchase.

ii) That the bus interests outside the City limits, or such other area as may be agreed with the Corporation, be operated by the Company or sold to the Western National Omnibus Company and other interested Companies, including the London Midland & Scottish and Southern Railways.

As part of the bargain, it has been agreed that the Corris Railway shall be transferred to the Great Western Company, free from all liabilities, for £1,000.[1]

Asset stripping is not a recent phenomenon. The Great Western was quick to recognise such possibilities, including the opportunity to control rival bus interests. Indeed, the Corris cannot have featured prominently in their strategy but the fact

34

that the little Welsh line also operated its own road motor services did not pass unnoticed. Much discussion took place at GWR Board level that year, culminating in a Memorandum of 10 October 1929, to the Finance Committee (Appendix III), undertaking to seek Parliamentary approval for the transfer of the line during the ensuing session. This was achieved in 1930 and the Great Western assumed full control of the Corris from Monday 4 August that year. Engine No. 3 emerged on Saturday, 2 August, to work the service on the last day of Corris independence.

There can be little doubt that the Corris held no particular appeal for the Great Western. It was always considered of little consequence, and it seems that GW officers at the Central Wales Division HQ at Oswestry, for example, were as much surprised as anyone by the acquisition.

That they were taken unawares and knew little of the topography or operation of the system is well illustrated by several requests for information, exemplified by the communication mentioned earlier regarding Llwyn-gwern siding, and by the following two examples. The first was sent to Machynlleth Low Level station from the Divisional Traffic Manager's Office at Oswestry as late as 28 October 1930, nearly three months after the GW had begun operating the line:

Slates ex Brach Goch (*sic*)
I understand that slates are quarried as above and brought down by road motor to Machynlleth L. L. Please let me know the exact situation of this quarry and how far from the nearest rail connection, stating exactly in which direction it lies from the particular station.

Engine No. 2's career was drawing to a close when it was stored in the open behind the carriage shed at Machynlleth. This clear image, dated by the retailer as 1925, reveals that No. 2 was reasonably complete at that time and, indeed, may not have been taken out of service much more than a year or eighteen months previously. Later photographs exist, taken in April 1926 and April 1927, which suggest that it is most unlikely that it was ever used after this period. The 1927 photograph,* particularly, reveals that cannibalisation for spares had clearly taken place by that time and No. 2 ended its days, finally, when it was towed to Maespoeth by the Kerr Stuart on 20 October that year, and parts were used to re-build No. 3. 1925.

(*See p. 70 *Railway Through Talerddig*)

Real Photographs

I presume there has been no siding connection at any time and it would be helpful if you could give me some particulars of the output, and also the class of traffic quarried . . . [2]

The second illustration is provided by the following Urgent Train Message sent to Mr Hamer, Relief Clerk at Machynlleth, on 29 August 1930:

Will you please let me know by next train without fail, what is the normal position of the public level crossing gates on the Corris Branch, and also whether it is the practice to couple up the side chains on all stock, as well as the centre coupling. [3]

Notification, 'by next train', that there were no side chains on the Corris stock probably surprised the District Traffic Manager's Officer at Oswestry but these are by no means the only examples to survive which demonstrate the lack of awareness and preparation by the larger company. Whereas the powers at Paddington were obviously happy to accept the Corris in order to acquire the various tram and bus interests, it was left to local management at the Divisional Office at Oswestry to see to the details, causing them to persist with a series of rather basic enquiries well after the takeover was accomplished.

The Great Western allowed the passenger services to continue from 4 August until the year's end, also the bus service between Machynlleth and Aberllefenni. The progress of both was carefully monitored and Paddington was not slow to appreciate the obvious popularity of the road motors. The people of the Dulas valley opted overwhelmingly for progress in the form of the modern bus, which obligingly carried its passengers to and from the centre of the town.

It is perhaps understandable, although regrettable, that no attempt was made by the GWR to persevere with the railway passenger service, even during the summer tourist season. There seems little doubt that had the people of Corris expressed some degree of support for the train, the services could have been retained but in the circumstances it was cheaper and far easier for the GW to withdraw the passenger trains and sell off the bus interests. The latter went initially to the Wrexham based Western Transport Company, the predecessor in this district of the Crosville Company. The last passenger train ran on Wednesday, 31 December 1930.

. . . More eloquent than a thousand words.

GBJ Coll.

A copy of the Weekly Return for General Goods Traffic 27.12.1930.

GBJ Coll.

From its inception as a railway linking London and Bristol in 1834, the GWR embraced over 180 lesser companies during its long and colourful history; the acquisition of the Corris in 1930 was the final addition to that great railway.

Freight only: 1931 to 1948

After the trauma of events leading up to 1 January 1931, the Corris settled down to providing a weekday goods service. Inward traffic, mainly coal and smaller items ranging from parcels to sacks of grain or kegs of beer, continued much as before. Slates and slabs, predictably, formed the bulk of outward traffic, but quantities of moss also featured in the accounts from time to time through to 1948 (see Appendix V).

Staffing under the GWR was reduced to a total of five. Driver Humphrey Humphreys continued with his former duty, but now as driver-cum-fireman. When he was indisposed, his place was often taken by Evan Maldwyn Jones, of Machynlleth, the celebrated baritone whose musical prowess was acknowledged throughout Wales, and beyond. He had started on the Corris as a driver/fitter during the line's independent days but under GW management became the fitter responsible for all Motive Power Depot (MPD) Plant over a wide area, encompassing former Aberystwyth & Welsh Coast, Newtown & Machynlleth and Manchester & Milford territory. If Evan Maldwyn was unable to deputise, a driver and fireman from Machynlleth covered the duty. Some of these crews were 'mainline' in every sense and the sight of two sizeable enginemen shoe-horned into the narrow confines of a Corris cab created a lasting impression, in more ways than one.

The heart of the Corris in Great Western days—Guard Price Owen and Driver Humphreys. That a good proportion of the guard's duties were out in the open where he was at the mercy of the weather is indicated by the waterproof leggins worn by Price. It may not have been raining when the photograph was taken but it would appear that the morning had been decidedly wet! 5.6.1946.

R. C. Riley

Driver Humphreys' colleague of many years standing, Robert Price Owen, now became guard-cum-shunter/loader/pointsman and clerk. His pay was on par with a main-line goods guard, whereas Humphrey received the same pay as a main-line fireman—a minor but occasional source of irritation between footplate and van. When Price Owen was indisposed, he was usually relieved by one of the regular Machynlleth goods guards: Guard Tom Morris, for example, worked the Corris service on Monday, 16 August 1948. Corris station was manned by a porter-clerk and during the 1940s, Miss E. (Lizzie) Humphreys, (Driver Humphreys's sister) held office. Short in stature but sharp in her movements, she is still well remembered in Corris as she trundled the station hand-truck around the village, busily delivering or collecting the various parcels.

Bulkier deliveries in the area were distributed by the carter, Dafydd Roberts: the horse was kept in the old Corris stables and the cart was usually parked behind the station. Dafydd Roberts and the horse also undertook some of the shunting on the tramway section, in the vicinity of Aberllefenni quarry.

Just one person, Lengthman Teddy Jones, was responsible for the track. Indeed, the condition of the permanent way was a legacy from the independent days which stood the Corris in good stead for the remainder of its existence although, as might be expected, reduced standards of maintenance encouraged a return to nature along the track. Sadly, the only green shoots of recovery evident on the post-1930 Corris were the verdant grasses which re-established themselves with a vengance where they had previously ruled for centuries before the coming of the tramway. However, the Corris was fortunate that sleepers

A fine demonstration of track relaying during the 1940s, and a good example of the skill of Teddy Jones who obviously knew what he was about. Indeed, to apply the term 'relaying' to the Corris during this period was something of a misnomer, for the supply of new rails was long exhausted; 're-sleepering' was a more accurate description, but the finished result was track of a surprisingly high standard. c.1947.

LGRP

and rails remained basically sound and faithful to each other, providing a smoother, more secure passage than might be imagined from a casual glance at the grass-grown track.

This situation must be attributed equally to the care bestowed on the track by Teddy Jones, who performed minor miracles with the limited resources at his disposal. When, for example, a rail fractured near the site of the Matthew's Mill turnout in the late 1940s it was replaced, not from stock, but by shortening the only siding on the system which could yield suitable material. This was the former arrival/departure line at Machynlleth, used after 1930 for holding the van overnight and for final assembly of the train before departure for Corris. This siding lacked a stop-block of any description after 1930, but its western end was protected beneath finely crushed slate waste; not so much a sand-drag as a slate-drag! Thus the fine waste

obscured the only source of rail available for redeployment in an emergency. The section of rail eventually relocated near the Matthew's Mill siding was not the first nor last to be removed; by 1948, several lengths had been retrieved from this source and redeployed elsewhere.

During the mid 1930s, Sir Henry Haydn Jones of Tywyn, owner of the Bryneglwys Quarry and the neighbouring Tal-y-llyn Railway, secured a lease on the Aberllefenni Quarry. Indeed, it appears that Sir Haydn's affection for the narrow-gauge proved a key factor in the survival of both Tal-y-llyn and Corris lines. Whilst it is not surprising that he actively supported the Tal-y-llyn, it seems that the Corris also benefitted from his love of the diminutive, for he constantly exhorted quarry customers to accept delivery by rail rather than road.[4] There now appears little doubt that Sir Haydn's assiduous support of the line during

The large tree growing out of the embankment carrying the line some thirty feet or so above the meadow also obscures the site of Rhiwgwreiddyn quarry, so near yet so far from connection with the Corris. Traffic from this source had first to be taken by cart to the nearby siding at Esgairgeiliog.

A light haze drifts from No. 4's chimney as it approached the photographer on a fine day in August 1935. H. F. Wheeler then used his new Leica camera to secure a second photograph as No. 4's trim little train waddled past him towards Esgairgeiliog. 12.8.1935.

H. F. Wheeler, courtesy R. S. Carpenter

the 1930s, helped by the optimistic projections of the local administration, enabled the Corris to survive a difficult period. Wartime circumstances prolonged matters for a time but, sadly, post-war recovery did not materialise and survival into the preservation era just eluded the little line.

As the line was then operated on the principle of 'one engine in steam', the signalling arrangements of the passenger era were allowed to lapse, although the signals and associated equipment were not removed until the wartime drive for scrap metal, *c*.1940/1. In addition to the removal of the signals and signal-boxes,[5] the opportunity was taken to reduce the runs of point rodding, and points were modified for local control. At first, the new ground levers were padlocked when not in use (Price Owen being the principal key holder) but, within a few years, the practice of locking the points overnight had gradually fallen into disuse. In addition to the signalling equipment, the 1940/1 scrap-drive also claimed the wagon weigh-table at Machynlleth, as well as the passenger run-round loop, the siding onto the old Ratgoed/ERA wharf, and the corrugated-iron carriage/bus shed. The smaller bus shelter attached to the station building at Machynlleth survived, and was leased during the 1940s to a local coal merchant for garaging his delivery lorry.

These changes represented the most obvious effects of the war on the Corris, although another consequence of hostilities was that No. 4 returned from overhaul *c*.1940 with segments of the cab windows painted with the special mustard-coloured substance calculated to change colour and give visible warning in the event of an aerial gas attack. In this respect, the Corris engines were treated equally with their standard-gauge counterparts.

The Kerr Stuart was off-loaded from the main-line wagon, probably on a Sunday, with the help of the local MPD's 12T hand-crane. In order to

View across the Dyfi valley, leaving Machynlleth. The signal cabin is minus glazed windows and the permanent way is being gradually over-run by meadow grasses; only fishermen making their way to the river and the inhabitants of the railway house at Ffridd Gate, taking a short-cut, keep the centre of the track reasonably clear. 5.7.36.

S. W. Baker

The interior of the Machynlleth western signal cabin. Most of the levers are identifiable: 1. Disc, 2. Home, 3. Car. Shed, 4. Points, 5. Spare, 6. ?. 7. Home, 8. Spare. 12.8.1935.

H. F. Wheeler, courtesy R. S. Carpenter

The original location of this lever frame is not apparent. On the evidence of another photograph taken the same day, this frame could not have been removed from the west cabin and it seems unlikely that it was taken from the east cabin as other photographs of this box exist—possibly of this era although they were undated—which show the levers in situ. By the appearance of the brambles and pronounced coating of rust, this frame may have been abandoned on this site, on the eastern side of the weigh table, for several years. It is more than likely that it was finally removed during the scrap drive of 1940-1. 12.8.1935.

H. F. Wheeler, courtesy R. S. Carpenter

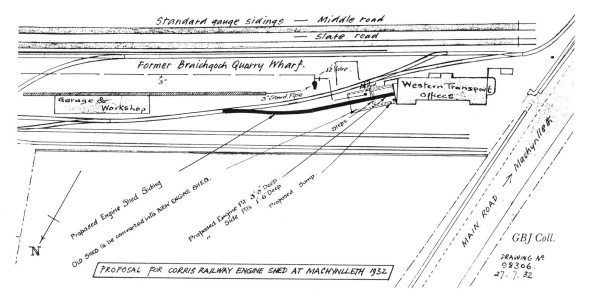

Standard gauge sidings — Middle road

— Slate road

Former Braichgoch Quarry Wharf.

12 Valve

Western Transport Offices

Garage & Workshop

3' Stand Pipe

Hyd.

Steps

Proposed Engine Shed Siding

OLD SHED to be converted into NEW ENGINE SHED.

Proposed Engine Pit 3'.0 Deep
Side Pits 1'.6 Deep

Proposed Sump

MAIN ROAD → Machynlleth

N

GBJ Coll.

DRAWING Nº
98306.
27. 7. 32

PROPOSAL FOR CORRIS RAILWAY ENGINE SHED AT MACHYNLLETH 1932

facilitate the process, the full length of both the 'slate' and 'middle road' standard-gauge sidings had to be cleared of other rolling stock—no simple matter at a time of intense rail traffic. No. 4 was swung across from the 'Crocodile' well wagon, to rest on the steel-rail locomotive siding behind the Low Level station; the coal-transfer siding immediately adjacent to the standard gauge at this location was laid with bridge rail, from which the Corris engines were prohibited.

The intention was to tow No. 4 to Maes-poeth at the end of the following day's work but this proved impossible as the brakes had been locked-on hard at the factory, probably as a secondary precaution whilst in transit, and could not be released on the Monday by Driver Humphreys who normally attended to such matters. No. 4 thus remained on the siding for several days until one of the main-line fitters was diverted from more pressing duties to rectify the matter. Thereafter, the Kerr Stuart returned to regular service and undertook most of the duties until 1947; No. 3 came out occasionally but did not really capture the limelight again until the final months of operation.

When the country was threatened by invasion during 1940, the precursors of the Home Guard, the Local Defence Volunteers (LDV) were most active. One of their first duties in the area was to establish a series of strategically located checkpoints on main roads. These were manned during the darkest days of the war but as the threat of invasion diminished, they were removed. One such post was located near the summit of Bwlch Pennal, on the Aberdyfi road, where a straight and substantial tree trunk could be lowered to form a barrier. Another was established near the motor-bus entrance to Machynlleth Low Level. In this instance, the post comprised two barbed-wire barriers placed in 'staggered' positions on the main road. Full advantage was taken of the proximity of the Corris Railway inspection pit which, with the judicious addition of a few dozen sand-bags, found itself serving as a useful slit trench.

The period of the Second World War saw vast tonnages of high explosives stored in the caverns of Braich-goch quarry. The 'powder', as it was generally referred to locally, was brought by rail into the lower yard at Machynlleth and there transferred to unmarked road vehicles for the journey to Corris. Had the Upper Corris branch been restored and upgraded in the 1930s, as the GW at one time contemplated, the explosives might well have gone by narrow gauge. Special

Two of the Corris drams in 1935, sporting a grey livery which they carried throughout the GW era (with the exception of odd planks on one or two wagons repaired during the 1940s and painted with a single coat of what might have been bauxite brown, which faded rapidly).

The grey livery as applied to the steel sided wagons seemed to retain its density over the years, whilst the same colour applied to the wooden bodied wagons appeared to lighten with time and weathering. 12.8.1935.

H. F. Wheeler, courtesy R. S. Carpenter

No. 3 passes over a stretch of fairly recently re-sleepered track, near Abergarfan. This photograph is also a tribute to the careful way Price Owen stacked the coal in the wagons. It is not difficult to visualise much of the load spilled on to the permanent way if the wagons were handled roughly and the load assembled carelessly. c.1947/8.

F. E. Hemming, courtesy C. C. Green

The widening of the formation of the line at Llwyngwern, to accommodate the siding to Llwyngwern quarry, served to present the writer with a fairly respectable 3/4 view which would not otherwise have been possible at this location. This photograph was the first of a short series taken that day. The writer was able to cycle ahead of the train to Maespoeth, where the bike was left in the shed during a return footplate trip to Aberllefenni. Only six exposures were made: all were successful but the number, although respectable enough by the roll-film standards of the time, seems pitiful in comparison with present day excursions which can easily devour half-a-dozen 36 exposure films!
9.7.1948.

GBJ

The main deficiency in the design of the little Falcons is well demonstrated in this 1948 action-shot of No. 3 breasting the Maespoeth bank, with the invaluable aid of Price Owen and a can of dry sand—a graphic example of local working practices which had no place in any official Working Time Table or Rule Book: indeed, the whole practice was so bizarre there was not even a rule prohibiting it! Wild flowers carpet the permanent way without quite managing to obliterate the turnout into Maespoeth shed. 9.7.1948.

GBJ

vans would have had to be constructed, but the cost could have been justified by their ability to work directly underground.

During this period, the post and tube fence at the entrance to the Corris station, bordering the footpath between the retaining wall and the former siding extension to the Abercwmeiddew wharf, began to decay. It was helped on its way by the driver of the coal merchant's lorry who 'converted' the 4ft pathway into a broader carriageway—with the lorry's assistance—merely to avoid travelling between garage and coal yard via two gateways and a short stretch of main road![6] The name-board located above the entrance to this footway, which served to guide passengers from the former Cambrian (later High Level) station, had been removed previously, during the early 1930s.

There is little doubt, however, that one of the most interesting proposals to materialise during the war years emerged in May 1943, when Cllr W. P. Evans suggested to the Machynlleth Urban District Council that passenger services be re-instated on the Corris Railway. Even at that dark hour, Cllr Evans obviously felt the Corris line had a role to play. He was reported in the local press:

> Its re-opening now would also help to provide better travelling facilities for the people of Corris and District as, owing to war-time conditions, the bus company could not be expected to provide more facilities. Passenger facilities on the Corris would also save road transport and petrol.

It was resolved that Mr Clement Davies MP and Sir H. Haydn Jones MP be written to, and that Merioneth County Council, Machynlleth Rural District Council, and Talyllyn Parish Council be asked to support representations urging that the Corris Railway be re-opened.[7]

Once more, regrettably, local support was lacking. The people of Corris again opted for the bus service and the proposal was carried no further. Regardless of other considerations, it must be granted that the prospect of the long walk from the station into the town of Machynlleth remained an important factor.

No. 3 pauses momentarily during shunting at Machynlleth, before setting out for Aberllefenni. 5.4.1948.

T. Alfred Hughes

Operating procedures: 1931-1948
A typical working day described

The shunting manoeuvres of the GW era could frequently appear somewhat haphazard to a casual observer, yet they were soundly based on the experience of decades and followed a regular and constant pattern. The brief description attempted here will be more meaningful if read in conjunction with the map on page 34, on which various points referred to in the text in square brackets [] are indicated.

The working day at Machynlleth usually commenced when Price Owen free-wheeled his way to work on a bicycle of great antiquity and dubious fidelity: normally, this occurred just after 8.00 a.m. Preparations for the day's trip up the valley almost invariably involved the transfer of parcels and other merchandise from the High Level station. This was usually achieved with the help of a specially designated 'Machynlleth Low Level Station' hand-truck. Other duties might include sheeting-over some perishable goods in an open wagon, or dealing occasionally with optimistic individuals who just turned up hoping for a trip along the line. A privileged minority sometimes appeared armed with indemnity forms and official passes!

When the service was reduced from six to three days per week, in October 1943, Price Owen used the non-operating days to transfer coal to the Corris wagons. If the demand was heavy, this operation would be continued on the morning of the service day, as was the practice during the period of six-day working.

Sometime around mid-morning on a service day, Price would have strolled toward the cross-over and wedged a suitably sized piece of slate under the point lever to enable the engine to coast in directly alongside the coaling 'stage'[A]. This could occur at any time between 11.30 a.m. and noon—times were always a bit vague on the Corris —but the tempo of the morning's proceedings always quickened a little with the appearance of the engine.

No. 3 pushes a pair of loaded slate wagons on the Aberllefenni wharf. The drop-side private-owner wagon next to the engine was a rare example on the Corris, at that time. 22.3.1948.

One of the final manoeuvres of a normal working day; No. 3 shunts empty coal wagons towards the crossover, and the coal transfer siding. Wagon 31987 was obviously in use at this time, but within three months or so it was proclaimed unfit for traffic. Note the leather Cash pouch protruding from the Guard's pocket; it would have carried a brass plate engraved 'GWR Corris'. 22.3.1948.

GBJ

Driver Humphreys's day would have commenced at Maes-poeth around 7.00 a.m. with the process of lighting the fire and raising steam. When relief footplatemen were required from Machynlleth, they had to make their way up the valley by the early morning Crosville service, leaving variously around 6.00 a.m.

After filling the engine's saddle tank from the water stored inside the shed itself—a great convenience during cold weather—Driver Humphreys usually left Maes-poeth around 11.00 a.m. for the quiet and gentle run down to Machynlleth. The driver had his own set of keys for the level crossing gates at Pont Ifans (Evans' Bridge), Llwyn-gwern and Ffridd Gate.

The engine usually travelled 'light' although it is believed that on occasions, during 1940, it called first at Corris, to pick up a few wagon loads of slates. This working is not explained in any official document, and it is not known where the loads originated, nor why they were brought down by the engine before the time of the service train. A possible solution, given the severity of petrol rationing at the time, is that the slates were delivered to Corris station by the railway horse and cart, from Braich-goch Quarry the previous evening, but a more feasible explanation, perhaps, could be that the loaded wagons came from Aberllefenni, and had been left in the loop the previous day as the weight of the train was considered excessive for the curves and gradients to Machynlleth.

The Great Western's Service Timetable stipulated that the maximum number of loaded slate wagons (categorised as Class 1) allowed between Aberllefenni and Machynlleth was 15[8]. Whilst the train might have been within the permitted load, the staff responsible for its safe passage to Machynlleth could have decided to leave a few loaded wagons at Corris as a precaution, for the Appendix to the Service Timetable from March 1943 (the closest publication date to 1940 available to the writer) states:

In order to ensure the train being under complete control during the journey over the varying gradients from Aberllefenni to Machynlleth the Guard will be responsible for seeing that the brake on one in every four loaded wagons and one in every eight empty wagons is securely applied before the train leaves Aberllefenni and these must remain on until arrival at Machynlleth.

The train must be brought to a stand at Maes-poeth when additional brakes must be applied as required by the Driver and after proceeding to Evans' Bridge Level Crossing these should be released.

Immediately on the Machynlleth side of Ffridd Gate Level Crossing the train must again be brought to a stand and sufficient further brakes applied to control the train to Machynlleth.

As the regulations imply, the section from Corris to Machynlleth was more hazardous than that from Aberllefenni to Corris and if the rails were particularly greasy, the option of leaving a few wagons in the loop at Corris until the following morning had much to commend it. The operation could thus be completed with greater regard to safety and the loaded wagons would still be available for transhipment at Machynlleth on schedule. The whole procedure possibly exemplified local arrangements of a kind which were once fairly commonplace on the railways of Britain: they could be executed in perfect safety, but featured in no Rule Book.

A more frequent variation on the 'light engine from Maes-poeth' routine was provided occasionally by the presence of an empty coal wagon towed down in the morning. This would have been used at the shed to store loco coal for lighting-up purposes. More comprehensive coaling of the engine always took place at Machynlleth, certainly during the GW era, where a small coaling stage

No. 3 at the Machynlleth coaling stage, viewed from the former Braichgoch wharf. The loaded coal wagons which had been run down previously from the coal transfer siding, have been eased back to allow the engine to be coaled, whilst a corner of an empty 'Maespoeth' wagon is just visible in front of the engine. The rather delapidated corrugated-iron shed had served as a garage for the road motors, and was considered as a home for the locomotives in a Great Western proposal of 1932. Had this been adopted, a mains water supply would have been provided virtually at the camera point. Note the selective cleaning of the saddle tank; obviously, it was not considered worthwhile to clean the parts not normally seen by the camera! 22.3.1948.
W. J. Keith Davies

was made by removing part of the rear wall of the Braich-goch wharf, at its western end.

The coal stage itself calls for a brief description. It comprised a grounded van body—latterly a GW iron mink—which was located on the wharf, roughly equidistant between the standard-gauge, to the south, and the narrow gauge to the north: it

Driver Humphreys chats with David Kenneth Roberts, grandson of Driver William Roberts, after drawing up at the coaling point at Machynlleth. Note the empty 'Maespoeth' wagon brought down that morning and also the carefully loaded wagon behind the engine. 7.6.1948.

GBJ

was elevated about three feet above the Corris metals. Coal was acquired from a standard-gauge wagon on the one side, stored in the van until required, then dispensed through the opposite doors to the narrow-gauge engines. Both sets of doors on the store were constantly locked when not in use although the central roof sections of the van had been removed in order to control the dust. All appeared secure from ground level and few realised the greater part of the roof was missing.

The engine would approach Machynlleth on the main running line and negotiate the cross-over before easing gently alongside the coal stage at [A]: this normally represented the limit of loco-motive working along this particular siding. Any loaded coal wagons for Corris were always run down the slight incline from the transfer siding before the engine arrived. This was much preferred to the alternative of running the loaded wagons

down after the engine's arrival at the coaling point for, under these cirumstances, the weighty dumb-buffered coal wagons could deliver a pronounced and uncomfortable blow, possibly dislodging some of their load in the process.

Coaling-up at Machynlleth was undertaken by Humphrey, for he additionally undertook the duties of coal-man, fire-lighter, steam-raiser, fire-dropper and ash-man; he was a one-man loco-motive department. Water was obtained at Maes-poeth during both 'up' and 'down' journeys.

Coupling and uncoupling were usually the res-ponsibility of the guard but as this was the Corris, the strict boundaries of demarcation were not always acknowledged. After coaling the engine, the driver frequently paid a visit to the main line Loco Stores for basic supplies of oil, cotton waste or sand. This latter commodity was carried in a special can which was used for filling No. 4's sand

50

boxes or, if No. 3 happened to be in use, for dispensing sand directly on to the rail, as the little Falcon was not equipped with any sanding gear (see photograph p. 45).

On his return from the Stores, Humphrey would draw the loaded coal wagons forward on to the goods loop to [C], simultaneously pushing ahead any empty loco-coal wagon which might have been brought down from Maes-poeth that morning. This would then be uncoupled and left at this location until later in the afternoon.

The short but tortuous route mid-way along the wharf initially served a dual role; in previous years, it was used to gain access to Braich-goch wharf as well as serving as the exit line from the neighbouring Aberllefenni area, a role it fulfilled to the end. Although it was laid with steel rails, the small radius reverse curves prohibited the use of locomotives, and horses would have been used on this section.[9]

The empty slate or slab wagons on the Aberllefenni wharf were pushed manually to the old Braich-goch sector; the points were reversed and the empties helped down the inclined curves to join the loaded coal wagons and the engine. After making sure all was well clear of the wharf exit points [B], the entourage then set back and used the cross-over to gain the main line before setting-back finally on to the van at [D].

Thus the train formation was constant; the

A weekend view of Maespoeth shed, with the guard's van stored on the old carriage siding until the Monday morning, when it accompanied the engine down to Machynlleth to pick up the traffic of the day. The low-roofed stone building on the left housed the stores and mess facilities for the fitters and footplate staff during independent days.

The locomotives were normally stored beyond the arched entrance, whilst the small shed on the right was used during the passenger period as a repair shed for coaches, although it was incapable of accommodating the full length of a bogie carriage. It obviously saw little use after 1930, as indicated by the large pile of ash behind the van. 21.7.1934.

F. M. Gates, courtesy R. C. Riley

51

Engine and van were rarely coupled together in this manner; the only regular occurrence was during the period of six-day working when, first thing on Monday mornings, the van was brought down from the shed by the 'light' engine. This view by F. M. Gates thus provides a sequel to his photograph of the van at Maespoeth. Humphrey and Price Owen were joined on this occasion by Iorwerth Hughes, from the main Loco stores at Machynlleth, who seems to be the bearer of an official message. 21.6.1937.

F. M. Gates, courtesy of R. C. Riley

loaded coal wagons were always next to the engine, and any empty quarry wagons were always next to the van. The same train formation applied to all goods trains, whether loaded or empty, whether running in the 'up' or 'down' directions, i.e., the GW coal wagons were at the Corris end of the train, whilst quarry wagons were always at the Machynlleth end. Sometimes, the train could consist entirely of coal and general traffic; on other occasions the load might be composed solely of slate or slab cars.

Before Braich-goch traffic ended in 1927, some quarry wagons were run down from the wharf directly into the coal transfer siding, where coal would be loaded for use in the quarry. Latterly, the trailing junction here was protected by a wooden scotch arm, which was normally padlocked

against the 'empty' Braich-goch traffic; it was installed when the signalling arrangements were rationalised during the early 1940s but served no useful purpose and saw no regular use.

The train could leave Machynlleth at any time after 12.30 p.m., but it was often nearer 1.00 p.m. before it was finally under way. Apart from the level-crossings, the first stop would be Maespoeth or Corris, where loaded coal wagons were drawn off the train by means of the engine and a rope. The small coal wharf at Corris, although well located at the northern end of the loop line, was used less frequently with the passing years. When the carriage shed became redundant in 1931, it found a new lease of life as a more convenient and secure coal store.

Shunting at Aberllefenni was not particularly

complicated; basically, the engine ran around its train which was then pushed onto the tramway section for the company's horse to draw away any full coal or empty slate wagons, and replace them with loaded slab cars or coal empties for Machynlleth. The process was made slightly more awkward during the final years as the inspection pit, located in the loop-line, was deemed unsafe to take the weight of the engine. This difficulty was overcome by organising a set of manoeuvres which did not require the engine's presence in the loop. The first requirement was to bring the whole train to a stand on the main line, alongside the platform and beyond the loop; it was then set back into the loop so that the van and a few of the empty slate wagons passed over the pit but stopped short of the points at the southern end. The engine was then able to run around on the main line and extract the whole train from the southern end of the loop, to push it back eventually along the main, on to the tramway section.

Here, the wagons were dealt with by the horse. When all had been removed, the van was returned by the engine to the southern end of the loop. The engine was then free to return to a point just short of the junction of the steel rails and the lighter bridge rails used on the tramway to Cymerau and Ratgoed. In due course, the horse would return with loaded wagons which were coupled up to the engine; any empty coal wagons were attached last. The engine then drew its train below the loop where the van, aided by gravity, would be run down to join the new formation.

At Corris, on the return trip, any empty coal

No. 3 near the limit of engine working at Aberllefenni; the steel rails gave way to the lighter tramway metals in the vicinity of the fifth wagon. The lack of a serviceable pit at the northern terminus at this time is demonstrated by the prostrate form of the driver between the rails, as he oils the engine's trailing wheels. 9.7.1948.

GBJ

The Kerr Stuart somehow failed to generate the same degree of affection as the Falcons, or at least, so it might seem from the various unsightly modifications it has been subjected to over the years. The practice continued even on the Talyllyn, where it carried the efficient though aesthetically disastrous Giesel ejector for many years.

One of the modifications carried out at Maespoeth during the mid 20s resulted in unsightly splash guards being fitted beneath the saddle tanks. These were intended to counter lazy or careless filling of the saddle tank, which obviously caused the motion to run hot after the excess water had flushed much of the lubrication away—a good example of curing the symptom rather than the cause.

Having run round its train at Aberllefenni, No. 4 takes a brief rest before the easier return down the valley; a respite which was well-earned if the over-heated smoke-box is any indication. 1925.

Photomatic

wagons were picked up from the old carriage shed. Occasionally, and in order to save a little time, these could be coupled behind the van, i.e., on the north or Aberllefenni side.

Apart from mechanical advantages of loaded wagons always being next to the engine—a significant factor on such a tortuous route—further

benefits of this arrangement were revealed on arrival at Machynlleth, where the train ran directly on to the goods loop-line, coming finally to rest when the last loaded slate wagon was clear (i.e., to the west) of point [C]. Here, the engine would be uncoupled. Any empty 'Maes-poeth' wagon left in the goods loop earlier in the day would now be

54

No. 3 on a 'down' train of two slab cars, two empty coal wagons, the van and a further pair of coal wagons, one of which carried a tarpaulined load, crossing the Dyfi on the final stage to Machynlleth. April, 1948.

GBJ

to the west of the engine, and automatically helped towards point [A] as the locomotive ran ahead to negotiate the cross-over and run around its train. Despite the relaxed atmosphere and general air of delapidation which pervaded the Corris during the final Great Western years, it was a surprisingly efficient concern in its own little way and its ergonomics were quite sound, given the equipment of the day.

After running around, the engine then drew off the van and any GW goods wagons, which were left briefly on the main line in the vicinity of point [E]. The engine's attention then returned to the loaded slate wagons in the loop, when two or three at a time would be extracted and pushed energetically on to the Aberllefenni wharf. This could be a noisy and most entertaining spectacle, particularly during wet weather, or during spring and summer, when the luxuriant grasses along the permanent

way lubricated the rails to such good effect. Transferring even a modest two-wagon load on to the wharf under such circumstances frequently generated great excitement and, indeed, was often not achieved at the first attempt. When the task was finally accomplished, the engine returned to the van and empty GW wagons; the latter would be shunted over the crosssing and deposited somewhere near point [A], and the van pushed to its normal stabling point at [D].

On Fridays, the engine was left near the site of the old west signal cabin whilst the driver walked to the High Level Booking Office to collect his pay and afterwards, perhaps, enjoy a cup of tea in the adjoining Refreshment Rooms. The day closed with the engine's departure for Maes-poeth, around 4.30—5.00 p.m.

The Saturday service, operated until 1943, calls for a brief explanation. The 'up' train operated

55

Few photographers recorded the transhipment of slates and slabs at Machynlleth but Stanhope Baker considered the operation to be sufficiently interesting.

Usually, only one man was employed on the wharf in GW days—William Breese, here with his back to the camera —but when a large consignment of slabs had to be transferred, further assistance was drafted from Aberllefenni. Just three weeks from closure, there was obviously sufficient work to warrant the presence of a second man to help with the task of manhandling the heavy slabs.

On the standard gauge, the grounded Dean 40ft Passenger Brake, immediately behind the two figures, stood on the site of the original cattle pens at Machynlleth whilst the adjacent coal wharf was used occasionally by the Co-op. The two engine sheds which form a grey backcloth to this scene are virtually bereft of chimney vents at the time of the photograph. The roofs, particularly of the older N&M shed (on the left), were then in a poor state of repair and had to be renewed during the early years of BR tenure. The Cambrian shed roof (on the right) was removed completely around 1966 and the walls were demolished during the Spring, 1993. 30.7.1948.

S. W. Baker

only as far as Corris that day and, as far as can be ascertained, only coal, parcels and an empty wagon were normally conveyed on Saturdays. The empty slate traffic, unless it was particularly heavy, usually remained at Machynlleth until Monday. On arrival at Corris, the coal wagons were placed in the old carriage shed before the engine, van and one empty wagon returned to Maes-poeth. The van was put into the short siding here (which formerly served the small carriage repair shed) until Monday morning, when it

accompanied the engine to Machynlleth. Price Owen then climbed into the empty wagon and with the engine's help, was pushed to the top of Maes-poeth bank; gravity and a judicious hand on the brake did the rest, enabling Price to reach Machynlleth and finish work for the day around 2.00—2.30 p.m. This somewhat bizarre arrangement was frivolously dubbed by colleagues 'the Corris's half-day'!

There never appeared to be a need for Price to work any overtime and he finished work around

No. 3 pauses after the day's work, at the location of the old west signal box at Machynlleth, before returning 'light' to Maespoeth. 5.6.1946.

R. C. Riley

No. 3 photographed at the same location, before making its way to Maespoeth as a light engine for the last time in the railway's history. No. 3 was stabled at Machynlleth at this time, but the previous day's boiler examination was not conclusive and the use of a pit was considered essential to complete the exercise. No. 3 simmered alongside the waving grasses for the better part of half-an-hour, before Humphrey emerged from the High Level station to drive it home to Maespoeth for its final visit. 9.7.1948.

GBJ

5.00 p.m. each day, although it was noticeable that home-ward progress at the end of the afternoon was markedly slower than in the morning, for in addition to weariness caused by the day's labours, he had now to contend with the effect of gravity as well as friction as he laboriously cranked his ancient steed up Heol y Doll.

The Corris remained a close-knit and friendly line to the end. During the GW period, unofficial passengers were surprisingly commonplace, and even complete strangers were made welcome provided the crew detected a genuine interest in the little train. Local enthusiasts were obviously well placed to avail themselves of this hospitality and a trip on the train was always a special treat; none more so than a journey on the engine back to Maes-poeth at the end of the day, which more than compensated for the return 4½ mile walk home.

Chapter 2: Notes & References

[1] *RAIL* 253/673.

[2] GBJ Coll.

[3] ibid.

[4] *Railway Magazine*, March 1988, pp. 180/1: 'Corris Conservation' by Richard Greenhough.

The later naming of the two Corris locomotives on the Tal-y-llyn Railway, after Sir Haydn and his manager Edward Thomas, is thus even more appropriate than was, perhaps, originally appreciated.

[5] 2 at Machynlleth and 1 each at Maes-poeth and Corris—with ground frames to control signals at the various level crossings and at Aberllefenni.

[6] During a visit to the derelict lower goods yard at Machynlleth on 28 March 1993, in company with Richard Greenhough of the Corris Railway Society, some short sections of bridge rail were discovered *in situ*, just beneath the road surface alongside the footpath which formerly connected the Corris and Cambrian stations. Later excavation by members of the Corris Society revealed a short section of the 1877 extension to the former Abercwmeiddew wharf and also an acute but most interesting spur which permitted the shunting horse to draw wagons into the main yard, and replace them on the narrow gauge with ease, after loading away from the Corris lines.

[7] *Montgomeryshire Express*, 15 May 1943.

[8] No record is available of maximum train loadings in the 'down' direction, but loads of 14 mixed wagons were observed on several occasions on 'up' trains during the early 1940s.

[9] A reply from Machynlleth Low Level station (29 October 1930) sent to H. Warwick, District Traffic Manager, Oswestry, in reply to a query regarding arrangements for handling Braichgoch traffic at Machynlleth (before the GW take-over) states:

Transhipment to and from standard to narrow gauge waggons [*sic*] performed by quarry's men, weighing of up and down traffic by Co's men at this station and towing from weighbridge to quarry's wharf alongside mainline by Co's horse.

GBJ Coll.

Chapter 3

Nationalisation

Few expected that nationalisation of the country's railway system on 1 January 1948 would bring any signs of relief for the Corris Railway, although a handful of optimists nurtured the belief that if the line could survive a few more years, the administration of the new 'people's railway' might yet appreciate its potential and induce a change of fortune. After all, the Great Western had successfully restored the Vale of Rheidol after suspension of services during the war, and it was just possible that the 1943 proposal to reinstate Corris passenger services, if only for tourists, would stand a better chance of success during the more buoyant post-war years.

Traffic from the quarries improved during the early months of the year but this was not difficult after the almost disastrous half year to December 1947, when a wages dispute forced Aberllefenni quarry to close. However, it was too soon for any dramatic upturn in the construction industry to be reflected in increased demand for slates and slabs, and even the tonnages of the early 1940s, modest as they were, were not repeated. Furthermore, two additional factors emerged during the ensuing months which directly affected the Corris; one of them ultimately contributed to its fate.

The first consideration was the condition of No. 4's firebox. This had deteriorated during the summer of 1947, causing No. 3 to be pressed once more into regular service. Boilersmiths travelled down from Oswestry Works during the summer and examined the Kerr Stuart at Maes-poeth, which resulted in the engine remaining out of service pending the decision of a higher authority, and No. 3 soldiered on alone, to the end.

The major cause for concern, however, was the manner in which the River Dyfi had been allowed to wreak havoc with the fertile meadows between the Corris Railway bridge and Craig-y-bwch, about ¾ mile up river. There is ample evidence that the Dyfi frequently changed its course over

the centuries, and several traces of ox-bow lakes remain between Cemaes and Derwen-las: the Corris itself negotiated one such feature, about mid-way between Machynlleth station and the river bridge, at a point generally referred to as 'The Culvert'. Indeed, the county boundary formerly followed the old river bed at this point.

The process of erosion, once under way, was gradual but inevitable and quite predictable. The river's change of course did not happen overnight but occurred over many months, most noticeably during periods of high water: between times, a *status quo* existed for weeks on end. Yet the river's advance was allowed to continue unchecked throughout the summer, autumn and winter of 1947, destroying acres of excellent pasture and causing the loss of hundreds of tons of fine soil.

It became obvious during the spring of 1948 that it would be only a matter of time before the river's meanderings posed a direct threat to the railway. The fact that the Railway Executive accepted the situation and intended taking no action to save the line was revealed when No. 4 was brought down from Maes-poeth one day after normal service and shunted slowly onto the siding directly behind the station at Machynlleth. It was joined by steel-bodied wagon No. 31987, which had also been recently condemned, and by No. 3. The date, regrettably, was not recorded but both Nos. 3 and 4 were well established at their new stabling point during June 1948, and Driver Humphreys performed the 'light-engine' part of his duties to and from Corris, by Crosville bus.

The apparently simple manoeuvre of stabling the Kerr Stuart at the end of the steel-rail siding was not accomplished without some difficulty. Moving slowly, cab first, No. 4 successfully negotiated the facing points on entering the siding, but the worn flanges of the small trailing wheels of No. 3 together, one suspects, with an accommodating check rail opposite the toe of the crossing,

Spring sunshine in the attractive Ffridd Woods warmed the photographer's back as No. 3 coasted into view around the curve and drifted, almost soundlessly, to a halt opposite the camera.

The two white pegs on the right of the picture marked the leafy and ill-defined edge of the embankment which here carried the railway some 15 ft above the feeder for the nearby mill—a salutary reminder of the perils of attempting a broader view.

All the writer's photography at this time was conducted with the aid of a humble box camera, with fixed aperture and shutter speed. Choosing the correct film to match the lighting conditions of the moment was thus a prime requirement, and as the shutter operated at a slow and unknown speed, only static subjects could be tackled with any degree of success. No. 3 was still moving when this photograph was taken, albeit slowly, so the camera was 'panned' in an attempt to match the speed of the engine. This technique was also used for the photographs of the train at Llwyngwern and approaching Maespoeth. The results of such a chancey venture, however, could not be determined until the film was processed, but the immediate reward in this instance was a footplate trip back to Machynlleth.
5.4.1948.

GBJ

The ground-level transfer siding at Machynlleth. Standard-gauge coal wagons are on the extreme left with a narrow-gauge counterpart alongside, standing on bridge rails. The locomotive siding, on the right, was at a slight angle to the standard-gauge siding and was laid with steel rails to accommodate the heavier loads. This photograph was taken around 08.00 and clearly shows the boiler being emptied for examination by the boiler inspector. 8.7.1948.

GBJ

This view of the erosion at the Dyfi river bridge also illustrates the early stages of the Ffridd Gate incline. 30.7.1948.

S. W. Baker

Although the river had been restored to its old course when this photograph was taken, periods of flood saw high water re-claiming the area of destruction which caused the closure of the line almost five years previously. Further erosion had undoubtedly taken place within that time but it is sad to reflect that closure was such a borderline affair.

The southermost pier has been removed by the river authority but the eastern wing of the nearby abutment has collapsed and lies partly submerged. April 1953.

GBJ

Two boiler-smiths travelled down from Oswestry during the summer of 1947 to see if repairs to No. 4's firebox were feasible; they completed their journey to Maespoeth by train but posed with Humphrey and No. 3 before departure. 1947.

GBJ

ensured that the trailing wheels of the Falcon rode up on to the vee-rail. That this was not a new problem was obvious from the driver's reluctance even to venture over the offending crossing. A heated discussion ensued amongst the assembled staff. The difficulty had obviously been encountered previously, probably when No. 3 had had to enter the siding to deliver and collect No. 4 for transfer to/from standard-gauge wagons in 1940. According to Driver Humphreys, the little Falcon was strictly barred from using the crossing.

There was little option, however, but to proceed with caution. Had the wheels actually left the road, help would have been readily available from the main-line breakdown gang, although the driver obviously wished to avoid any such embarrassment. On the first occasion, the offending flange rode on the rail for the better part of a yard, before dropping into place. Fortunately, the Falcon's driving wheels caused no concern and No. 4 was pushed to

the end of the steel rails. As No. 3 had to be stabled on the same siding, the 'performance' of negotiating the crossing was repeated at the close of each working day. With familiarity, the driver's consternation was dispelled until the hazard eventually became mere routine and was treated in a more casual, almost blasé manner. In some inexplicable way, the offending pony wheels seemed to 'behave' themselves progressively with each fresh entry into the siding, and the distance travelled by the flange along the rail's surface diminished as the weeks passed. There appeared to be no sign of deterioration of the steel rail; it can only be assumed that the general wear of the offending flange on the crossing caused some mysterious improvement in its performance.

Thus the little line approached the end of its days. Traffic during July was not heavy, certainly nowhere near 14 wagons witnessed earlier in the decade but it was respectable enough, with an

A Crosville version of the Corris Railway's Road Motor Service c.1952. Leyland-engined GA15 stands outside the Depot at Machynlleth, directly above the diesel storage tank let into the forecourt c.1941. Previously, all buses at Machynlleth were petrol-driven; the change-over was a gradual process. c.1952.

Anon. GBJ Coll.

63

A spacious new depot was constructed by the Crosville Company at Machynlleth in 1934; it lay directly across the route of the former Derwenlas/Morben tramway. In this 1953 photograph, the depot was decorated for the Coronation of HM The Queen. By a strange twist of fate, Crosville left the site in 1991 and the buses at Machynlleth have reverted to their former haunts at the Corris Railway station. The 1934 depot remains empty at the time of writing, whilst the buses are stored in the open. c.June 1953.

Anon. GBJ Coll.

average of around half a dozen in most trains. A good day would see seven or eight wagons in the train, reflecting, to some degree at least, a little of the optimism expressed by the local staff.

The river, however, continued its destruction of the meadowlands unchecked, until it eventually threatened the southern approach to the bridge. The lethargy of the river authority was difficult to comprehend at the time but the inertia was obviously welcomed by the Railway Executive which quickly realised that by matching the tardy attitude of the river authority, the embarrassment of the Corris would soon be easily and permanently removed. Had the Railway Executive so decided, the threat of a breach could have been averted with ease even at the eleventh hour, simply by transporting quarry waste in its own wagons from

Aberllefenni, where it was freely and abundantly available, to the very spot where it was required.

A final irony concerned the two locomotives for, even as the crisis at the river bridge approached its climax, a boiler inspector travelled down to assess the condition of both locomotives. After the inspector's appraisal, the writer sought an unofficial verdict. Quite why that officer should confide in a complete stranger is not apparent but he divulged that No. 4 would be recommended for a heavy overhaul, 'So there will be one good engine': the words struck a strangely optimistic yet anachronistic note. Inspection of No. 3 was attempted at Machynlleth on 8 July but as a full examination required the use of a pit, the new stabling point at the terminus was abandoned briefly on the 9th, to allow one final overnight visit to the old home at

Maes-poeth, where the examination was completed the following day. It appeared that No. 3, whilst also in need of a good overhaul, was to be recommended for light repairs, sufficient to allow it to serve adequately as a stand-by engine. Regrettably, neither the inspector's name nor HQ were noted, but his report may still survive amongst the official records at the PRO: it would be interesting, one day, to learn if it followed the unofficial, verbal account.

Owing to the ever-increasing proximity of river and railway at the approach to the bridge, it required no great powers of perception to sense that the end was imminent, even before the Dyfi burst its banks again over the weekend of 21/22 August. The following Monday morning dawned bright and sunny; the flood showed signs of abat-

ing and a visit to the station became necessary to discover the extent of any further erosion, or to learn whether the train would once again be permitted to venture up the valley.

The pace of life at the Low Level station could hardly be described as hectic at the busiest of times, but there would usually be some sign of activity by mid-morning on a normal operating day. At 11.30 a.m. on 23 August 1948, however, there was no evidence of Guard R. P. Owen loading parcels into the van nor was Driver Humphreys to be seen 'coaling up' or busying himself around the engine. The slide bars and piston rods on No. 3 had been oiled, as though for the day's work, but the fire-box was cold. The canvas fastened across the cab at the end of each working day was still in place, although now embellished with a recently

No. 4 at its last resting place on the Corris. Although it was securely sheeted over, Price Owen was usually willing to peel the canvas back to reveal the Kerr Stuart for the benefit of interested photographers. Wagon 31987 was also condemned at this time, when it was discovered that the steel body and the wooden solebars were separate entities; corrosion had completely destroyed the securing bolts. 30.7.1948.

S. W. Baker

David Kenneth Roberts poses with the sheeted No. 4 at Machynlleth, seemingly gift-wrapped for the Talyllyn Railway. 7.6.1948.

GBJ

chalked inscription—'Not to Be'. Was the anonymous writer interrupted, perhaps, as he attempted to chalk the well known Great Western locomotive legend, 'Not to be Moved', or did he reveal a poetic awareness and sense of occasion often unsuspected of those who regularly perform manual tasks? The enigma will remain, but the three simple words which prevailed on the canvas for several weeks, until gradually obliterated by the summer rains, presented a poignant and, until now, very private epitaph to the old Corris Railway.

The decision to suspend the service was probably taken by Mr Campbell Thomas, the Machynlleth Station Master, though precisely when it was announced is not recorded. But the die was cast; the Corris would run no more. Official confirmation followed in September.

It was defeated not only by its one-time ally the river, as is most frequently asserted, but also by the lack of initiative and determination demonstrated by those in authority. The easy option of closure was welcomed; an option which, regrettably, was to be seized all too readily in the ensuing years as countless branch lines were annihilated by the fateful combination of road competition and unenterprising, often defeatist, management.

The trackbed directly beneath the rails was never fully breached. Almost magically, or so it seemed, remedial work to restore the river to its former course was undertaken soon after the closure was officially declared. This was achieved well before 1953, when the RAF photographed the valley. (See p. 15).

The Aftermath

On reflection, it somehow seems appropriate that only the engine and van travelled down the line on Friday, 20 August 1948. This was a rare event in itself, but quite extraordinary that it should occur on what transpired to be the last day of operation. It thus so happened that by pure chance the Corris/GW/WR rolling stock was all at Machynlleth that weekend and even the three Private Owner wagons which had arrived on Wednesday, 18 August, had all been neatly returned on the final 'up' trip of Friday, 20 August. It was almost as though the whole exercise had been carefully planned but it was, in fact, no more than one of the little coincidences which occasionally touch all our lives.

Several good accounts of how the neighbouring Tal-y-llyn Railway profited from the demise of the Corris have previously appeared in print; there is little point in repetition here other than, perhaps, to suggest that had not the Corris locomotives, wagons, van and steel rails been available to the infant Tal-y-llyn Railway Preservation Society at that time, the success of that venture and the advancement of railway preservation in general could have been jeopardised. Indeed, it could be argued that without the Corris transfusion, and gestures such as the Hunslet repair of engine No. 4 in 1951, the Tal-y-llyn project would certainly have been much retarded and might well have foundered ignominiously. The significance of such matters, however, tends to recede with time and, although not without some interest, is now only of rhetorical relevance.

Locomotives 3 and 4 were purchased for £25 each, loaded on to a GW standard-gauge wagon

No. 3 leaving Corris metals for the last time. This snapshot, by an unknown photographer, was discovered amongst the writer's father's papers. Preparations for the move obviously involved clearing out the old ballast to verify the state of the sleepers. Staff in attendance are J. H. James, Chargeman Fitter and P. Smythe, Fitter's Mate, Machynlleth MPD, and Station Master Campbell Thomas.

Anon. GBJ Coll.

Back to nature: Aberllefenni station site twelve years after closure. The station building has now been demolished and a service road cuts across the site, to houses built on the left of the picture. 8.8.1960.

WIMM

(Crocodile F, bogie well wagon No. 41937) and sent to Tywyn on 17 March 1951. The total rail charge, including cranemen's wages, hire and haulage of the crane amounted to a mere £30.12*s.* 9*d.* The goods brake-van was purchased privately and donated to the Tal-y-llyn Railway. It was sent to Tywyn on the 7.40 a.m. Goods from Machynlleth on 7 April 1951, and the rail charges amounted to £8.6*s.*11*d.* Finally, eleven goods wagons followed in July that year; the charge for the latter, 'delivered to Towyn [*sic*], carriage free' was £16.10*s.*2*d.* Thus the Tal-y-llyn acquired the Corris Railway rolling stock, including delivery to Tywyn, for just over £100; an incredible bargain, even by 1951 standards.

The best of the rail and pointwork also found further use on the Tal-y-llyn, although a small quantity was transferred back to the Dulas valley for re-laying by the Corris Society in 1971.

The bridge over the Dyfi was dismantled during late December 1948—early January 1949, the steel-work being stored for many months at Machynlleth, on the old Aberllefenni transfer wharf. Shortly after removal of the main girders the southernmost masonry pier developed a decided list. All three masonry piers appeared to have a somewhat shallow foundation, suggested by the broad bed of rubble-based concrete which surrounded each base. The wooden piles which edged this area had rotted away over the years, allowing scouring of the foundation. The masonry thus dislodged presented considerable resistance to the flow of the river, and as a consequence, was speedily demolished by the river authority, in direct contrast to their reaction to the earlier erosion problem.

The horse-worked tramway to Cymerau and Ratgoed continued in use until 1952, whilst a section of the original tramway, between the quarry and the cutting sheds at Aberllefenni, survived into the late 1970s; motive power at this late date being provided by a conventional tractor which straddled the rails. As a result of the 1948 closure, BR introduced small open containers, not unlike the original wagons in size and capacity, for carrying the slates and slabs. The containers went by road and eased the problem of transhipment at Machynlleth quite considerably but their introduction was too late to be of any benefit to the railway.

The old wharves at Machynlleth thus saw no further quarry traffic but those used formerly by the Ratgoed and Braich-goch companies were used during the 1950s by the local GPO Telegraph Depot, for the storage of new telegraph poles. This practice continued for several years, until advances in telephone technology reduced the need for pole storage on such a scale.

The deterioration of the Corris Railway buildings accelerated rapidly after the closure. Machynlleth Low Level was still used for a time as the meeting place of the old GW Staff Association and it survives today as a base for a successful cycle hire business, whilst the adjacent garden centre occupies most of the Corris land to the north of the former running line. The buses left the site in 1934 when

Although No. 4 left the Corris for Tywyn on 17 March 1951, it paid another visit to the lower yard at Machynlleth, on 21 February 1952, when it spent a brief period between arrival on the coast goods and departure on the last 'up' goods of the day to Oswestry. It was destined for Hunslets of Leeds, where the engine was given an overhaul at no cost to its new owners. In order to facilitate the work, No. 4 was partly stripped down at Tywyn, and travelled in that condition; boiler cladding, parts of the cab and saddle tank etc., accompanied it in an adjoining wagon. 21.2.1952.

GBJ

New surroundings, new friends; Corris No. 4 inside the repair shed at Tywyn (Pendre) in company with TR No. 1 Talyllyn. Neither engine was in running order at that time. 13.8.1951.

GBJ

No. 4 and Price Owen's van head a passenger train at Abergynolwyn, on the Talyllyn Railway, shortly after the Kerr Stuart's return from Leeds in working order. Apart from acquiring an unglamorous name and detail differences, No. 4 appeared much as it operated on the Corris. At that time, even the buffing and draw gear were unaltered. Summer 1952.

GBJ

the new Crosville depot was built (across the path of the former Derwen-las tramway) just south of the GWR line to the coast, but they have since returned to their former haunts on Corris land as a result of the transfer of the 'new' depot building in 1991. They currently use the site of the old tramway stables, providing a further ironic twist to the Corris story.

The station buildings at Llwyn-gwern and Esgair-geiliog also survive, having been refurbished and adapted as bus shelters. Those at Corris and Aber-llefenni, on the other hand, had deteriorated rapidly and were demolished largely in the interests of safety. Maes-poeth shed alone maintained any industrial connection after the closure and was used by the Forestry Commission. Since 1981, it has once more fulfilled its original role as the workshop of the Corris Railway.

The final chapter is provided by the formation of the Corris Railway Society in 1966 (see Appendix VI). It has successfully established a museum in the old railway stables at Corris, and relaid the track between the site of Corris station and Maes-poeth shed. None of the original rolling stock has

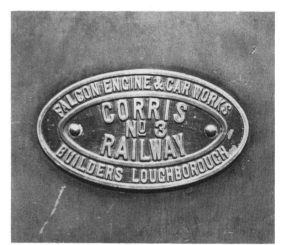

The right-hand numberplate carried by No. 3, which probably dates from its rebuilding in 1900. The original Hughes works and number plate was also oval in shape but slightly smaller in size. The photograph was taken in the engine siding at Machynlleth. 30.7.1948.

S. W. Baker

The right-hand number plate originally carried by No. 4. During its first nine years on the Corris, it was always known by this number but bore no evidence of that fact until the figure 4 was fashioned in steel by the GWR and rivetted on to the brass plate soon after the GW take-over. The legend, 'No. 4047 1921, originally in raised brass figures and located horizontally across the centre of the plate, had to be removed to make room for the new '4'. The works number and date, however, were not lost but stamped onto the lower rim.

LGRP, courtesy R. C. Riley

been returned for use in the valley, although part of one of the Corris coaches, sold in 1930, and the saddle tank of No. 3 have returned as museum exhibits.

A second coach saved from the scrapman in 1930 has been restored at Tywyn and operates on the Tal-y-llyn Railway. The brake-van has been completely rebuilt by the Tal-y-llyn; the small, oval Falcon Works buffers were replaced at an early date and the whole body was later condemned and removed to serve for a time as a shelter at Quarry siding, between Dôl-goch and Abergynolwyn. The wood- and steel- bodied goods wagons were particularly useful during the reconstruction of the Tal-y-llyn; both the engines have been restored by their new owners and, during the process, considerably rebuilt and altered in appearance. It becomes increasingly difficult for anyone who can recall the engines making their way vociferously across the Dyfi to Ffridd Gate, or

The Corris coach rescued from a garden at Gobowen and beautifully restored at the Pendre Carriage works of the Talyllyn Railway, was photographed at Tywyn the day following its initial trial run and before it entered service. 23.5.1961.

GBJ

struggling to heave wagon loads of slates and slabs on to the wharf at Machynlleth, to visualize them as Corris engines today, and it is astonishing to realise that they have now been on the Tal-y-llyn for over 42 years. No. 4's Tal-y-llyn Railway service, for example, already exceeds its period on Corris metals by 12 years.

The Nos. 3 and 4 of the 1990s now seem to belong in the salty air of Tywyn and alongside the little Afon Fathew; despite the 2ft-3ins track once more running south of Corris, it is most unlikely that either engine will ever again see the inside of Maes-poeth shed.

Although it was not appreciated at the time, only three weeks remained before closure. Despite the encroaching vegetation, No. 3 battles through with its mixed train of coal, general merchandise, empty quarry-wagons—and unofficial passengers—on 30 July 1948.

S. W. Baker

Appendix I

Extract from *Oswestry Advertiser*, 25 July 1860

Machynlleth: Fatal accident

An accident of a melancholy nature occurred on the 11th inst. near the station of the Corris & River Dovey Tramroad, close to our National Schools. The contractors for the conveyance of slates and flags from the Corris quarries along the tramway allow their driver (whether right or wrong, we know not) to convey passengers occasionally down on top of the load for a 'trifling consideration', and on the day above named Mrs Elizabeth Jones requested permission to come from her residence about 3 miles in the country, to the station at Machynlleth.

Within about 100 yards [of ?] she alighted, when the trains [*sic*] were in motion, and walked incautiously along a low, dilapidated walk running parallel with the rails, and in reaching for her basket, which was left on the carriage her foot slipped, and her clothes became entangled in the wheels, by which means her right leg was lacerated in a frightful manner. Several parts of her body were much injured. Mr G. Owen and Mr Lloyd, surgeons, were soon on the spot, and her leg was subsequently amputated by those gentlemen. She only survived the operation a few hours, and died the next morning. The deceased was a widow of about 57 years of age and had kept a fulling mill in the neighbourhood for many years.

On the 12th inst. an inquest was held at the Skinners' Arms, before Capt. Lloyd, Coroner of the District and a respectable jury, and the coroner laid the following queries before the jury for their consideration.

1. Are the regulations and practices on this tramway sufficiently preventive to ensure safety?
2. Does the company allow persons to be conveyed on this tramway?
3. Does the company enforce the law to prevent children and others from using, for their own diversion, the trains on Sundays?

After hearing the evidence, the jury returned a verdict of 'accidentally killed by having the right leg fractured by the wheel of a tram carriage.'

Appendix II

The following is a slightly rearranged copy of the rough draft of a letter to Sir Clifton Robinson. It is neither dated nor signed, but is accompanied by a separate list of the quarries on which a few additional notes are added in another hand. This information was incorporated within the main letter and suggests that the separate list, which bears the date 22 November 1909, may well have formed the initial draft. In the interest of clarity, some of the entries have been juxtaposed to conform with the original writer's own headings, a) to d). It is more than likely that the letter was the work of J. J. O'Sullivan.

With a few notable exceptions, such as the map and traffic statements for 1902 and 1908, it appears reasonably complete and the hand-writing in both ink and pencil is, for the most part, easily readable. The author's additional notes, focussed mainly on the few examples of illegibility, are in square brackets.

Dear Sir Clifton,

As requested by you I have now pleasure in sending herewith map of our line showing all the various Quarries on it, as far as I can. Also a statement showing the output of these quarries during 1902 and 1908. I have numbered all the quarries as you will perceive on the map, and propose to deal with them in the following order.

a). Quarries in which trial openings only have been made.
b). Quarries worked and closed.
c.) Quarries closed and re-opened.
d.) Quarries now working.

a)   CWMDYLLUAN:
Trial openings only were made here, but quarry was never worked. This is also the property of Mr Evan Thomas of Rhiwgwreiddyn, Esgairgeiliog.

GLYN IAGO:
Trial openings only have been made here. Whose property?

RHOGNANT:
In this quarry only trial openings were made and it proved to be a continuation of the Gaewern vein. This quarry is the property of Mr D. Owen, London.

HENGAE:
Trial openings only have been made at this quarry. Whose quarry? Owen, Hengwrt, Dolgelly [sic]

FFYNNONBADARN:
Ditto.

GOEDWIG:
Trial pits LHVT [Lord Herbert Vane Tempest]

b)   TYNYBERTH:
This quarry is the property of Mr Evan Thomas of Rhiwgwreiddyn, Esgairgeiliog, and has not been worked for over 35 years. When worked it is stated that good slates and slabs were procured from it. The alleged reason of its having been closed was that a layer of spar was met with in the process of excavation, and apparently it was not considered prudent to quarry further there. All the rails, together with the plant that originally existed there has been removed.

TYNYCEUNANT:
This is the property of Mr D. Owen, Russell Gardens, Kensington, London and the same remarks as on [Tynyberth] apply also to this quarry.

ABERCWMEIDDAW [sic]:
This quarry is the property of the Ecclesiastical Authorities or Church Commissioners and had been worked up to March 1904 by the Company. In 21.3.06 an execution sale took place in which the plant and machinery, rails etc were removed, leaving nothing except the engine house and machine

shops, which are in a bad state of repair. The quarrymen who worked there state that the slates and slabs procured there were the finest in the district, and there is an abundant supply of water which was utilised for the purpose of driving the machinery. The slate produced there was of a silver-grey colour; there was almost an unlimited supply of rock.

BRAICH-GOCH & GAEWERN

The quarries are adjoining to one another and are the property of Lord HVT. They have been worked by the Messrs Buleys [?] or Bridges [?] up to 1906 since which time no work has been done there.

The Braich-goch quarry has been worked to the level of the existing machinery shops and was then discontinued as they would have to go furth[er] down. They consequently worked the Gaewern quarry up to the time of closing. The slates were dark blue from this quarry and were of undoubted good quality, and to continue working the Braich-goch on the same level would probably entail the making of a new tunnel in a westerly (?) direction or continuing to work the Gaewern Quarry in a northerly (?) direction beyond the bounds of LHVT and into Rhognant quarry which . . . purchased.

FRONFELEN:

This quarry is the property of the Manager of the Fronfelen Estate, Mr Badham, (Solicitor? of . . .) and has not been regularly worked for about 40 years, principally due to the fact that whilst there was abundance of stone and slate of a dark blue colour, the latter was found in course of time to fade into a dirty iron colour, and the quarry was apparently abandoned for that reason.

CYMERAU:

This quarry has not been worked for about 15 years and it is at present flooded. The pumping machinery is still there and the planing machinery etc are [sic] in the workshop, which shop is in a bad state of repair. The slates and slabs got were of good quality. This was also worked by water power. It is the property of Mr Owen of Hengwrt, Dolgelly.

CAMBERGI:

This was only worked for a short time and abandoned. Whose property? Mrs Anwyl, Penbontbren, Bow Street.

DARANGESAIL:

Worked and closed a great number of years ago, 40-50. Col. Ruck.

b) & c) & d)
ERA and CAMBRIA WYN:

These quarries are at present in possession of Mr Badham, the mortgagee who has sub-let them to a few quarrymen working in co-operation as a temporary arrangement for 12 months at £20 a year with rates. The stones from these quarries are used for slabs only, being too brittle for cutting up into slates, but they are reported to be very good for enamelling purposes, e.g. mantel-pieces etc. There is an abundant supply of water power for driving the machinery.

c) & d)
RHIWGWREIDDYN:
This quarry is somewhat similar to the ERA and is also worked by a few quarrymen in co-operation. It is the property of Mr Evan Thomas, who let it to the men at £60 per annum, which rent he has not enforced. This quarry is worked almost entirely by steam.

d) ABERCORRIS [sometimes referred to as Cwmodin]
This quarry is the property of a Mrs Davies A'th [Aberystwyth?] and is at present held on lease by J. Lewis of B'ham, who paid a rent of £125 a year for it, which rent has been reduced, I am informed, to £62.10.0 for some years past. At present the quarry is being worked for slabs only as the stone they are getting now is rather hard for slate. It is entirely worked . . .

LLWYNGWERN:
This is in the possession, I believe of Mr W. J. Lewis, who holds it on lease from Lord Herbert Vane Tempest, and I understand it has been assigned by Mr Lewis to a Mr S. Fowler Wright of B'ham, but on what terms I cannot say. The stone from this quarry is somewhat similar to that of the ERA and Rhiwgwreiddyn and is only used for slabs for enamelling etc. Both the slabs from this quarry and from Ratgoed and Abercorris are brought down to a small works close to our M'lleth station where they are enamelled and prepared for the market by Mr Wright.

ABERLLEFENNI:
These quarries are the property of Capt A. R. Pryce and are the only quarries which have a [record of] continuous working . . . they are worked by water power, of which there is an abundant supply.

RATGOED [corruption of the original name, Yr Allt Goed—The Wooded Hill]
This quarry is at present being worked by Mr W. J. Lewis, but in what manner held by him I cannot say, probably by lease (?). The sawing and planing machinery are [sic] all worked by water power, and the slabs produced are of good hard quality. None are now being turned to slates owing to the hard nature of the rock.

APPENDIX III

Memorandum to the [GWR] Finance Committee, 10 October 1929
(Rail 253/673)

In conjunction with the purchase of Shares of the Bristol Tramways and Carriage Co. Ltd., the Board on 15th February last authorised the acquisition of the Corris Railway undertaking for £1,000. The capital of the Company comprising £15,000 Ordinary Stock and £5,000 Debenture Stock is held by the Imperial Tramways Company Limited and it has been ascertained that on 28th February 1929, on which date it was understood the purchase would operate, the financial position was as follows:—

Purchase price	£1,000: 0: 0
Stock and Stores	1,100:15: 6
Accounts due to Company	476:12: 2
	£2,577: 7: 8

Less liabilities of the Company,
(apart from indebtedness to
Imperial Tramways Co. Ltd.) £2,369: 1: 3

Since that date a sum of £600 has been advanced by the Imperial Tramways Co. Ltd. to the Corris Company making the amount due £808: 6: 5.

It is proposed that in consideration of the payment of this amount to the Imperial Tramways Company, the Ordinary and Debenture Stocks shall be transferred to the Company and the Corris Company's indebtedness of £15,823:12: 5 to the Imperial Tramways Co., cancelled. In accordance with the directions of the Board, the stocks will be registered in the names of Sir Ernest Palmer and Mr F. R. E. Davis, as nominees of the Company, except £2,000 Ordinary Stock representing the Directors' qualification, which will remain registered in their names for the time being, and in respect of which Trust Deeds will be executed.

Parliamentary authority for the acquisition of the Corris Railway undertaking will be sought in the Bill to be promoted by the Company in the ensuing session of Parliament, and the Committee are asked to authorise the arrangement being concluded with the Imperial Tramways Company Limited on the above mentioned basis.

Appendix IV

i)   List of employees at 30 June 1901 (Not complete) (GBJ Collection)

Name	*Occupation etc.*	*Started*	*Previous engagement*
J. R. Dix	General Manager	1878	With Cambrian Rly. Co.
Wm. Morris	Corris Station Master	1883	With Mawddwy Rly. Co.
D. Thomas	Machynlleth S. M.	1890	At Llwyngwern Station
J. Roberts	Aberllefenney [*sic*] S. M.	1886	At the quarries
H. Davies	Llwyngwern S.M.	1893	In South Wales
Thos. Theodore	Esgairgeiliog S. M.	1894	At Rhiwgwreiddyn
Wm. E. Jones	Clerk, Corris	1900	None
E. Griffiths	Guard	1889	Quarries
Wm. Lloyd	Horse driver, Corris	1896	ditto
Wm. Richards	Horse driver, Corris	1896	Farm labourer
J. Jones	" " "	1899	—
J. Tibbot	" " Machynlleth	1881	None
J. Jones	Porter, Machynlleth	1883	At a Foundry
D. Owens	Signalman & Storekeeper, Maespoeth	1895	At Quarries
J. Rowlands	Porter, Corris	1900	ditto
E. R. Williams	Boy Porter, Corris	1898	None
R. Pattison	Engineman & Fitter	1886	On the Talyllyn Rly.
Wm. Roberts	"	1887	At the Quarries
Thos. Howells	Fireman	1899	None

Missing from the list:—
— Permanent Way workers
— Level-crossing gate-keepers

ii)   List of employees 1930, as listed, in random order (GBJ Collection)

Name	Occupation
E. M. G. Williams	Lad Clerk
Ed. Griffiths	Acting Porter, Machynlleth
H. Rowlands	
H. Edwards	
H. Humphreys	Engineman
E. M. Jones	"
H. Williams	"
H. B. Jones	Machynlleth Station Master
D. J. Roberts	Horse driver, Corris
G. E. Jones	Corris Station Master
Wm. Richards	Horse driver, Corris
Evan Griffiths	Guard
John Isaac Jones	Porter
W. A. Owen	Fitter (Buses)
C. H. Evans	Fitter
R. I. Roberts	Fitter (Buses)
W. E. Evans	
E. Blayney	Bus driver
R. L. Jones	
Edward Hughes	
E. M. Edwards	"
Rd. Holt	"
Wm. Edwards	"
P. Ward	"
Hugh Jones	"
Jack Evans	"
T. A. Hughes	Bus conductor
T. D. Hughes	Bus driver
J. L. Roberts	
R. Price Owen	Porter/Guard
Gwen Williams	Garnedd-wen Gate-keeper
M. E. Williams	Llwyn-gwern Gate-keeper
Mrs Griffiths	Ffridd Gate-keeper
D. J. McCourt	General Manager

— Permanent Way workers not identified.

— Approximately half the staff listed as bus drivers were actually bus conductors at this date. With the exception of T. Alun Hughes, who elected otherwise, all attained driver's status in Crosville days.

Appendix V

STATEMENT of Traffic dealt with at ESGAIRGEILIOG SIDING January—July 1930

Date		Consignee	T.	C.	Q	lbs.	Rate Description	£	s	d
Jany.	9th	Rowlands P. Office		2	2	23	S/c Groceries		1	7
"		Thomas, Rhiwawel		2	2	0	" Cement		1	5
	20th	Forestry Commission	4	4	2	0	6/- Live)	1	5	4
	23rd	" "		3	2	22	S/c Plants)		1	7
	25th	Pugh, Era Terrace		2	2	0	" P'toes		1	5
	"	Forestry Commission	3	1	2	0	6/- Plants		19	6
	"	" "		8	0	0	" Manure		2	5
	31st	Rowlands, P. O.		2	1	16	S/c Groceries		1	5
Feb.	6th	Forestry Commission	1	0	0	0	6/- Wire		6	0
	17th	Lloyd & Jarvis		5	0	0	S/c Lime		2	11
Mar.	1st	Forestry Commission	1	0	0	0	6/- Plants		6	0
	6th	Rowlands, P. O.		2	1	13	S/c Groceries		1	5
	"	Forestry Commission		2	0	2	" Drums Oil		1	5
	10th	" "		16	3	0	6/- Plants		5	0
	24th	R. H. Lloyd		3	0	0	S/c Bags Seed		1	7
	26th	Rowlands, P. O.		4	1	0	" Groceries		1	7
	26th	Forestry Commission	2	9	0	0	6/- Plants		14	9
Apl.	3rd	Rowlands, P. O.		3	3	23	" Groceries		1	4
	14th	I. Rowlands	1	0	0	0	5/6 Coal		5	6
	22nd	John Davies		2	0	0	S/c Bags Coal		1	4
	28th	Forestry Commission	1	3	0	0	6/- Rolls Netting		6	11
	30th	" "		15	0	0	" " "		4	6
May	1st	Rowlands, P. O.		3	1	19	S/c Groceries		1	7
	27th	E. Jones		4	0	0	" Coils Wire		1	7
June	26th	Rowlands, P. O.		3	1	14	" Groceries		1	7
	30th	" Minafon		1	0	0	" Bag Coal			10
July	18th	J. Davies		2	0	0	" Bags Coal		1	4
	24th	Rowlands, P. O.		3	0	22	" Groceries		1	7

T 18. 11. 0. 16.   £6. 3. 5d.

TRAFFIC TO ESGAIRGEILIOG SIDING

GBJ Collection

ii)

STATEMENT OF TRAFFIC dealt with at ESGAIRGEILIOG SIDING January—July 1930

Date		Sender	Description	Weight				Rate	Charges			To
				T.	c.	Q.	lbs.		£	s	d	
Feb.	1st	R. H. Lloyd	Bags of Moss		19	2	0	6/-		5	10	Birmingham
	17th	" " "	" "		14	0	0	"		4	5	"
	27th	" " "	" "		13	2	0	"		4	3	Wisbech
	"	" " "	" "		5	0	0	S/c		1	7	Manchester
	"	" " "	" "		5	0	0	"		1	7	"
	"	" " "	" "		11	1	0	6/-		3	5	Nottingham
	"	" " "	" "		3	0	0	S/c		1	7	"
Mch.	26th	" " "	" "		17	0	0	6/-		5	4	Birmingham
	"	" " "	" "		6	0	0	"		1	11	Crewe
Apl.	9th	" " "	" "		17	0	0	"		5	4	Birmingham
	26th	" " "	" "		7	2	0	"		2	1	Liverpool
	29th	" " "	" "	1	6	0	0	"		7	10	Wolverhampton
May	6th	" " "	" "		3	1	0	S/c		1	7	Solehull [sic]
June	25th	" " "	" "		15	2	0	6/-		5	3	Birmingham
	"	" " "	" "		3	2	0	S/c		1	7	Wisbech
	"	" " "	" "		11	3	0	6/-		3	6	Solehull [sic]
	"	" " "	" "		4	0	0	S/c		1	7	Crewe
	"	" " "	" "		4	3	0	"		1	7	Stockton on Tees
	26th	" " "	" "		2	2	0	"		1	5	Birmingham
				9	10	0	0		3.	1.8d.		

TRAFFIC from ESGAIRGEILIOG SIDING

GBJ Collection

80

Appendix VI

The Corris Railway, 1966 to date

The Corris Railway Society was founded in 1966, with the twin aims of studying the history of the railway and district, and opening a museum dedicated to the line. Following an unsuccessful attempt to purchase Machynlleth Station, the old stable block at Corris Station became the home of the Corris Railway Museum, with the first section opening in 1970. The Museum has been enlarged as repairs to the building made more of it useable, and is open during the holiday season and at other times by arrangement.

The first section of rail for a 'demonstration track' was relaid in 1971, close to the Museum. By the mid-1970s, the Society felt confident that it could reopen part of the line to passengers, and so incorporated the Corris Railway Company Ltd in 1977, to take over the railway side of the Society's operations, while the Society was registered as an Educational Charity.

Planning permission was granted for a line from Corris to Maes-poeth, and following negotiations

The new Corris Railway, June 1993. Works Manager Vince Roberts drives a train alongside Maespoeth engine shed. The end vehicle is a new passenger carriage built for the railway and based on the design of the original bogie vehicles. June 1993.

Tom Heatlie

81

with the concerned authorities, broad agreement was reached for a further two miles, to the Forestry Commission picnic site at Tan-y-coed. However, a 1981 planning application for this section was rejected, and lengthy discussions to amend this decision have continued ever since; at the time of writing (April 1993) a further application has been lodged and the situation appears promising.

Nevertheless, the Company acquired the sheds at Maes-poeth in 1981, and the remaining trackbed between there and Corris in 1984, so that since 1985 works trains have been able to run throughout this section. Since then the Company has concentrated on upgrading the track with heavier rail and building up rolling stock and equipment ready for the recommencement of passenger services, while awaiting permission to extend southwards.

The Society has undertaken extensive historical research, with the aim of producing a definitive history of the Corris. It has also published a number of works on the railway.

Richard S. Greenhough, on behalf of the Corris Railway Society   *April 1993*

Bibliography

BOYD, James I. C., *Narrow gauge Rails in Mid Wales,* (1986). Oakwood

BRIWNANT-JONES, Gwyn, *Railway Through Talerddig,* (1991). Gomer Press

CORRIS SOCIETY, *Return to Corris,* (1988). Avon-Anglia

COZENS, Lewis, *The Corris Railway,* (1949). Cozens

RICHARDS, Alun John, *A Gazetteer of the Welsh Slate Industry,* (1991). Gwasg Carreg Gwalch

SCOTT MORGAN, John, *Corris*, (1991). Irwell Press

Various issues of *Railway Magazine, Railways* and local newspapers, particularly *The Cambrian News, The Montgomeryshire County Times* and *The Oswestry and Border Counties Advertiser.*

Index